DUNE
AWAKENING

THE ART AND MAKING OF

Written by Andrew Farago

Foreword by Joel Bylos

Introduction by Brian Herbert, Kevin J. Anderson, Byron Merritt, and Kim Herbert

LONDON

CONTENTS

FOREWORD 9
INTRODUCTION 10
- LEGACY 14
- GENESIS 24
- REBIRTH 46
- THE WORLD OF ARRAKIS 64
- FOUNDATION 98
- THE SPICE OF LIFE 120
- TOOLS OF THE TRADE 134
- TRAVERSAL 152
- THE NATURE OF THE BEAST 182
- THE LONE AND LEVEL SANDS 190
- ARRAKIS ASCENDANT 210

ABOUT THE AUTHOR 218
FRANK HERBERT 220

FOREWORD

By Joel Bylos, Creative Director

Almost six years ago, I was invited to travel with a small group of developers to Budapest and visit the set where Legendary Entertainment and Denis Villeneuve were filming the first motion picture of the upcoming Dune saga.

At the time, I wasn't working on *Dune: Awakening*, but as a huge fan of the Dune books, I begged and cajoled my boss to allow me to tag along.

It's hard to describe how it felt to walk among those sets. Good movie sets are like portals. Walking through the halls of the Arrakeen palace, treading the hallways of an abandoned testing station, climbing inside an ornithopter—for me, each of these is a real memory of a real place.

Through the work of Denis Villeneuve and his team, I had visited the world of Dune.

So just over a year later, when I had the opportunity to join the *Dune: Awakening* project as creative director, I leaped at the chance.

Funcom is no stranger to building worlds—Arrakeen Palace from the Dune-adjacent world of Rubi-Ka in *Anarchy Online*, the shadowy cities and towns of *The Secret World*, the rich and vibrant world of Conan the Barbarian in *Age of Conan* and *Conan Exiles*. We've been doing this for a long time.

But Dune was different. A beloved universe with a fiercely loyal following and a set of blockbuster Hollywood movies that have taken the world by storm.

The pressure was real.

The team began with the original source. Teasing out the descriptions from the books, finding every obscure mention of location and object and character. Digging into the films, finding every frame of reference that we could.

The landscapes of Dune are expansive and epic, but they are desert. For players to spend hundreds of hours here, we needed to move beyond the desert landscapes of the films. We looked at dozens of desert landscapes across the planet—Wadi Rum to Death Valley to the Outback of Australia. We created specific biomes that were mentioned in passing in the books, and we imagined how the towns and villages of Arrakis would look based on the details that we could tease out from Frank Herbert's works.

Though the costume design of the films was award-winning, a video game requires a different approach: a progression in the sets to satisfy the needs of players. Our character artists set to imagining what it was like to begin your journey as a nameless prisoner, the lowest caste in the Imperium, and visualized every step of that journey: from the rags of a Maula to the robes of the Regis Familia.

Every world is the sum of thousands of details, lovingly crafted by our artists with a focus on trying to create the most authentic Dune experience for our players. Within these pages is a glimpse of the work that went into realizing *Dune: Awakening*.

As the great Frank Herbert once said, "The stories that are remembered are the ones that strike sparks from your mind, one way or another."

I hope that the art in this book strikes sparks in your mind. And that *Dune: Awakening* is a world worthy of remembering.

PAGES 2-3, 4 *Environmental landscapes exploring the colors and textures of the Vermillius Gap.*

PAGE 6 *Landscape scene showcasing the architecture of Carthag.*

OPPOSITE *Concept art exploring the environmental phenomena of Arrakis.*

INTRODUCTION

By Brian Herbert, Kevin J. Anderson, Byron Merritt, and Kim Herbert

Generations of Dune fans have been immersed in Frank Herbert's desert world of Arrakis, but now it's possible to experience the Spice-rich sands, the dangerous cities, the huge harvesters, the Fremen sietches, and the awesome sandworms in a whole new way.

Have you ever wished you could visit the dusty old city of Arrakeen? Or Harko Village, Hagga Basin, or the Deep Desert? Well, the new survival game *Dune: Awakening* takes you there! For years, dedicated Dune fans have been clamoring for a new multiplayer computer game based on the science-fiction masterpiece *Dune*.

It takes time to develop such an in-depth and expansive game, but the result is certainly worth the wait! Steam describes it glowingly as "A multiplayer survival game on a massive scale. Survive the sandworm, craft your ornithopter, build a fortress, and ascend to power on an open-world Arrakis."

Dune: Awakening is also a role-playing video game, a shooter game, an adventure game, and a fighting game, all with such attention to detail that it's sure to please even the most demanding fans. Developed by Funcom in collaboration with Legendary Entertainment and Herbert Properties LLC (Frank Herbert's estate), the game is playable on PC.

Imagine yourself standing atop a sand dune or in the Great Erg, watching the approach of Shai-Hulud. Here comes the mighty worm! Do you have the skills to survive the desert—or to escape the massive beast?

Frank Herbert's novel *Dune* has inspired millions of readers worldwide. He wrote five sequels expanding the story for thousands of years. Frank passed away in 1986, leaving the story uncompleted, and in 1999, his son Brian Herbert and coauthor Kevin J. Anderson picked up the mantle and wrote many more novels and short stories in the fantastic universe.

In 2020, Brian and Kevin began adapting the Dune stories into comic format. The first volume of *Dune: The Graphic Novel* was named one of the 100 Best Graphic Novels of All Time by Comics Authority. In 2021 and 2024, Denis Villeneuve and Legendary Entertainment brought *Dune* back to the big screen for moviegoers in two major motion pictures, and later, in 2024, the *Dune: Prophecy* series produced by Legendary Television for HBO Max streamed for television viewers.

Beverly Herbert, Frank's loving wife of thirty-seven years, championed new games and merchandise in the 1970s and 1980s, foreseeing Dune's future and recognizing the importance of the gaming space. Their granddaughter, Kim Herbert, remembers when she was only seven years old, how excited her grandfather was to show his grandchildren, Kim and Julie, along with their parents, Brian and Jan, the newly released Dune board game in the library of his Port Townsend, Washington, house.

In recent years, Dune tabletop and digital games have been developed, but *Dune: Awakening*—a multiplayer survival open-world crafting game (SOC)—is a significant expansion into a much broader form of entertainment, where fans around the world can imagine themselves interacting with and living in the vast and dangerous deserts of Arrakis. This will bring gameplayers into the Dune-fold in a very

ABOVE *A scenic landscape overlooking the Arrakis desert.*

PAGES 12-13 *Concept art exploring Atreides-style building architecture.*

modern way.

We hope that fans who first experience the Dune universe through *Dune: Awakening* will decide to open one of the novels and see what all the excitement is about. Start with the original *Dune* and go from there.

We think Frank and Beverly Herbert would be pleased to see how expansive the Dune universe has become, and that it continues to evolve in new and fascinating ways.

Brian Herbert (son of Frank Herbert) and Kevin J. Anderson are authors of multiple prequels and sequels to *Dune*. Kim Herbert and Byron Merritt are members of Herbert Properties LLC.

Frank Herbert's *Dune* is a landmark in science fiction. Since its initial publication in 1965, the original Dune novel has never gone out of print and has sold tens of millions of copies all over the world, in more than twenty different languages. Herbert's first sequel, *Dune Messiah*, was published in 1969, and additional novels—four more from Frank Herbert, more than twenty by his son Brian Herbert and Kevin J. Anderson—have built upon the foundation that he established in his original, visionary story of a distant future on the planet of Arrakis, a harsh desert world that was both alien and familiar, a cautionary tale of politics, environmentalism, fate, and destiny.

"By the early 1970s, sales of *Dune* began to accelerate, largely because the novel was heralded as an environmental handbook, warning about the dangers of destroying the Earth's finite resources," said Brian Herbert in his 2005 afterword to *Dune*. "Frank Herbert spoke to more than thirty thousand people at the first Earth Day in Philadelphia, and he toured the country, speaking to enthusiastic college audiences. The environmental movement was sweeping the nation, and Dad rode the crest of the wave, a breathtaking trip."

The novel became a cultural touchstone and influenced a generation of science-fiction writers and artists, as well as scientists and environmentalists. Despite several attempts to bring Herbert's epic to theaters in the 1970s, *Dune* did not make its way to cinemas until 1984, under the auspices of director David Lynch. A second adaptation, a three-part television miniseries, was produced by the Sci-Fi Channel in the year 2000. The most recent, a two-part epic, released as *Dune* and *Dune: Part Two*, produced by Legendary Entertainment and directed by Denis Villeneuve, who cowrote the screenplays with Jon Spaihts (*Dune* and *Dune: Part Two*) and Eric Roth (*Dune*), has become a true global phenomenon, as Frank Herbert's tale of political turmoil in a time of global crisis is more relevant than ever, over sixty years after the publication of his original novel.

PAGES 14-15 *Concept art of an Arrakeen courtyard.*

OPPOSITE TOP *The lower floor of an Arrakeen bar.*

OPPOSITE MIDDLE *The upper-floor balcony of an Arrakeen bar.*

OPPOSITE BOTTOM *The upper-floor relaxation area of an Arrakeen bar.*

The box office resurgence of Dune has brought with it a renewed interest in the expanded Dune universe, from novels, illustrated books, and adapted and original graphic novels to the television series *Dune: Prophecy*. As production commenced on Denis Villeneuve's first film, Legendary Entertainment knew that the time was right to embrace another aspect of Dune's history and made plans to develop the most ambitious Dune video game to date, a multiplayer SOC set on the planet Arrakis. *Dune: Awakening*, produced by the innovative studio Funcom, would continue a proud tradition of groundbreaking Dune video games dating back to 1992, when the first single-player strategy game set in Frank Herbert's universe was released on floppy disks and the new CD format.

"*Dune: Awakening* moved very quickly at Legendary. I approached partners at GDC [Game Developers Conference] in San Francisco and all the major gaming conferences, preselling Dune to potential partners," says James Ngo, Senior Vice President of Franchise Management at Legendary Entertainment. "All of the companies I spoke to went back to the core of the early *Dune* games. The low-hanging fruit is to make an RTS [real-time strategy game], and nearly every studio proposed that approach to Dune. It took a while for us to find a partner who had the same vision for the same games that we did, but once we met with Funcom, we knew that we had found the right team for Dune. It's a balancing act, finding the right way to use the IP."

Sam Rappaport, Legendary Entertainment's Vice President of Interactive Media, spent more than six years on *Dune: Awakening*,

working alongside Funcom and his Legendary colleagues. "There was some concept art from the film when I came on, but basically nothing really thought out about the game yet, other than it would be an open-world multiplayer survival game, because that's Funcom's bread and butter," says Rappaport. "We didn't know anything about the film's look or tone at the time and had to compile that as we went. We knew it would be something we hadn't seen before, and we wanted to stay faithful to Denis's vision for the franchise. If you look at the literary descriptions in the book, as well as other visual adaptations, those are different from what previous filmmakers envisioned, but we wanted to create something that would complement Denis's vision of Dune."

TOP The upper-floor entrance of an Arrakeen bar.

MIDDLE A hologram displayed in an area of the bar's upper floor.

BOTTOM The upper floor of the bar.

Legacy

ABOVE *Concept art of an Arrakeen plaza.*

Although the visual development of *Dune: Awakening* would mirror that of the films as established by Villeneuve and Production Designer Patrice Vermette, the game would be no mere film-inspired walkthrough, and Funcom made it clear from the very first production meetings that *Dune: Awakening* would provide a unique experience that would complement the films but would stand on its own as an expansion of Frank Herbert's beloved science-fiction universe. "This game is not meant to be 'play the movie.' It's inspired by the world that the movie has created," says James Ngo. "The visual designs, the color palette, all of that, it serves as the foundational source of our inspiration, but our game has to last longer than a two- or three-hour movie. We had to take some creative liberties along with Funcom to evolve some of this source inspiration in order to make the game into what it needs to be.

"How do we expand on this universe and bring a different perspective on it? We didn't want to be a mirror image of the movie; we always wanted to build on it and offer something unique. The game is so deep and so vast."

Dune: Awakening honors not just the recent film adaptations, but also the vast literary universe established by Frank Herbert, Brian Herbert, and Kevin J. Anderson over the course of more than two dozen novels, and, to an extent, the six previous video game adaptations that were played by many of the crew at Funcom and Legendary during their formative years. Paying homage to what has come before while charting a new course is a delicate balancing act, but one that the creative team relished. "Any project of this scale is not going to be without its challenges," Ngo continues. "Everything needs to fall in line from the top down, from two different companies. Aligning everyone from Herbert Properties, Funcom, Legendary, it took a lot of coordination, but we all believed in the potential of this game. We may have had different opinions, but we all had the same goal. Keeping that as our focus really brought us all together."

The heart of that focus, from day one, was the original *Dune* novel, and its author, Frank Herbert. "*Dune* was visionary, ahead of its time. And its themes resonate through history as well," says Ngo. "It endures because Frank Herbert was able to tap into human nature and psychology. The foundation of that house is so strong that it can be reimagined and interpreted by creators like Denis, and in such a beautiful way so as to keep it relevant and to shine the spotlight on Dune again. It resonates with people from a visual and a thematic standpoint."

Those complex themes were both a blessing and a curse when it came to *Dune: Awakening*, according to Barnaby Legg, Chief of Creative Marketing at Legendary Entertainment. "One of the great advantages of Dune as a science-fiction property is one of its disadvantages for a mainstream audience," says Legg. "If you are a science-fiction fan like we all at Legendary are, it's arguably the *War and Peace* of science fiction, right? It's an astonishingly powerful magnum opus of science fiction, which is so loaded with big ideas. The creation of a completely believable future. And with it, a level of complexity that goes beyond much of the sci-fi that we've experienced.

TOP *Arrakeen market vendors.*

MIDDLE, BOTTOM *3D renders of a sandworm statue.*

"Most people who love Dune love it for its complexity. The complexity of its world-building. The complexity of its cultural ideas. Its languages. This is a franchise where you need a glossary of terms if you want to understand what's going on. We have a hero, Paul Atreides, who goes by multiple names. Lisan al-Gaib. Muad'Dib. The Kwisatz Haderach. That shows you the expansiveness and breadth of the world that Frank Herbert created. On a surface level, that can be very alienating for non–science-fiction fans. A very big ocean to jump into.

"What we tried to do with the marketing of Dune, certainly with what Denis and screenwriter Jon Spaihts tried to do, which was brilliant with the film, was to bring out the things that relate to everyone, whether you're into science fiction or not. All the best speculative fiction is about humanity. Where we're going. The science fiction that breaks through represents the best of the genre, and what it can do at its best is to shine a light on who we are by imagining what we might become. Looking at a future version of ourselves, it's a story about humanity. It's not about alien races and strange creatures that we can't relate to; it's about us, ten thousand years from now. And I think that's something we'll always be fascinated by."

GENESIS

*D*une chronicles the life of young Paul Atreides, whose family's journey to the desert planet of Arrakis at the behest of their emperor sets in motion a series of events that will transform not only his life but also the fate of all Arrakis, and perhaps the entire universe itself. From birth, Paul had defied fate, as his mother, Lady Jessica, a member of the mystic order of the Bene Gesserit, bore a male child in direct opposition to the sisterhood and the Reverend Mother herself. Paul's prescient talents and use of Bene Gesserit skills indicated that he may be the prophesied Kwisatz Haderach, "the one who can be two places simultaneously," a male born of the Bene Gesserit whose mental powers can bridge space and time, and who will become one of the most powerful and influential leaders in the universe.

After the death of his father, Duke Leto Atreides, following a failed assassination attempt against his political rival Baron Vladimir Harkonnen, Paul and his mother must flee into the unforgiving desert and join the nomadic Fremen tribe of Arrakis. Paul Atreides adopts a new identity and takes a new name inspired by the adapted kangaroo mouse of Arrakis, a creature associated with the Fremen earth-spirit mythology, with a design visible on the planet's second moon. This creature is admired by Fremen for its ability to survive in the open desert, and the creature's name is reborn in Paul Muad'Dib. His abilities and his influence over both his adopted tribe and his father's people allow him to rise to power to unseat the Emperor Shaddam Corrino in order to take control of the known Empire itself, fulfilling the prophecy of the Kwisatz Haderach.

PAGES 24-25 *Concept art of the pain box room.*

OPPOSITE *Environmental designs of the pain box room utilized by the Bene Gesserit.*

LEFT *Sketches and concept design of the Reverend Mother's seat in the pain box room.*

Genesis | 27

But what if these events did not come to pass? What if Lady Jessica had not followed her heart but the dictates of the Bene Gesserit, and had given birth to a daughter instead of the Kwisatz Haderach of legend?

The answers to those questions set in motion the events of *Dune: Awakening*.

"In *Dune: Awakening*, Paul does not exist," says Sam Rappaport. "Lady Jessica gave birth to a daughter, Ariste Atreides, as she was supposed to. There are characters in the films and in the novels that are in *Awakening*, but the alternate history allowed Funcom the creative freedom to explore the look and feel of those characters but in a way that was inspired by but not exactly the same as the films."

The decision to explore an alternate history of Arrakis and Dune was not an easy one, but as soon as Funcom and Legendary hit upon it, they knew that it was the right one. "It's one of the things I'm proudest of that we did with the game," says Barnaby Legg. "We knew that we needed to find a unique approach to the story the game tells, because the game isn't a direct adaptation of any one of the novels, nor is it an adaptation of the movie. So the question came up early on, what is the story? And really, the key to that is we were talking to Funcom about this idea that in the universe of Dune, it's all about possible futures, right? The Bene Gesserit are doing this, Paul Atreides is doing this, the Mentats are doing this. Everyone is trying to look at every possible path to the future and find the one in which humanity survives. And early on, this idea came up of what if this is a game where everyone for themselves can decide just what this future should be.

TOP, BOTTOM *Early explorations of Shield Wall.*

"Paul Atreides, in the movie, as an example: once he has ingested the Water of Life, it opens his mind to every possible outcome of the future, all these different outcomes. And as he says, he has seen one narrow way through. So Funcom pitched this very clever idea of what if there was a split in the timeline? An alternate future in which Lady Jessica did not defy the Bene Gesserit and she did give them a daughter, and Paul Atreides was never born? And that was a very liberating pitch. Because firstly, it allowed us to embrace the canon but also create a canon. It's a unique magic trick, I think, that Funcom have pulled off that only a story world like Dune allows. It is a world in which we can go into parallel timelines and present it to the player as one of many possible futures. Which I think, cleverly, links into the players' experiences. The player wants the world and the universe they know, but they want it to be the sandbox for their story, that they want to tell. So the alternate timeline was a very clever way of doing that."

Joel Bylos, Chief Creative Officer at Funcom, is an expert on Dune lore, and he and his team had many spirited conversations about the ramifications of a world where the Kwisatz Haderach of legend does not rise to power. "I think what happens is that when there's no Paul Atreides, there is no clear hero to unite behind. People are fractured, and the world is fractured, in a sense," says Bylos. "The Fremen have found someone that they think may be someone like Paul Atreides, and, spoiler, it's not the player. They've been looking to fulfill this prophecy and are desperate to find someone to do that. There's a vacuum, and someone must try to fill it. The Fremen, in the game, they're not really there, but as you explore the ruins and where they used to live, you find out more information about this character they had thought might be the one.

OPPOSITE TOP *A scene depicting the Siege of Arrakeen.*

OPPOSITE BOTTOM *Concept art depicting remnants of the Desert War.*

LEFT *Concept art of the power transmission scene.*

"Paul's absence brings about a lot of space, and that leads to a lot of player freedom. If Paul were alive, everyone would rally behind Paul Atreides because he's the Kwisatz Haderach. But with him gone, that's not really how it goes. That gives us a lot of room for player freedom. And it asks the question, if there is this vacuum, what fills it, exactly? And if this war has been going on for ten years, a stalemate between the Harkonnen and the Atreides, what does that mean for the world itself? What has changed in that world? In the game, we have these scavengers who wouldn't be there because the Fremen would have kept them out of certain areas of the planet. But now the Fremen are missing, and the scavengers are there, because they can be. It changes the paradigm of the world and how it can be. Paul casts his shadow over everything.

"And Lady Jessica's dynamic changes with the Duke," he continues. "The fact that they have a daughter is interesting, since that means the Bene Gesserit have a much more vested interest in the House Atreides than they did in the movie and in the books, where their attitude is, 'if they live, they live; if they die, they die,' since they didn't really believe that Paul was the one. But in *Dune: Awakening*, they need the daughter because they need her to give birth to the Kwisatz Haderach, so

their opinions are much stronger and they are much more invested in what's going on, which leads to much more drama and political intrigue."

The removal of the most famous, most prominent character in all of Dune was a huge creative risk, but a necessary one, according to Funcom Producer Nils Ryborg. "Paul Atreides is one of the great characters in fiction, but ultimately, he is a force of nature. That makes any storytelling around him inherently unfun [from a gameplay perspective], because, unless the player is playing Paul Atreides, you will have no control of what's going on.

"We needed to remove Paul."

ABOVE *Environmental explorations and concept art of the Vermillius Gap.*

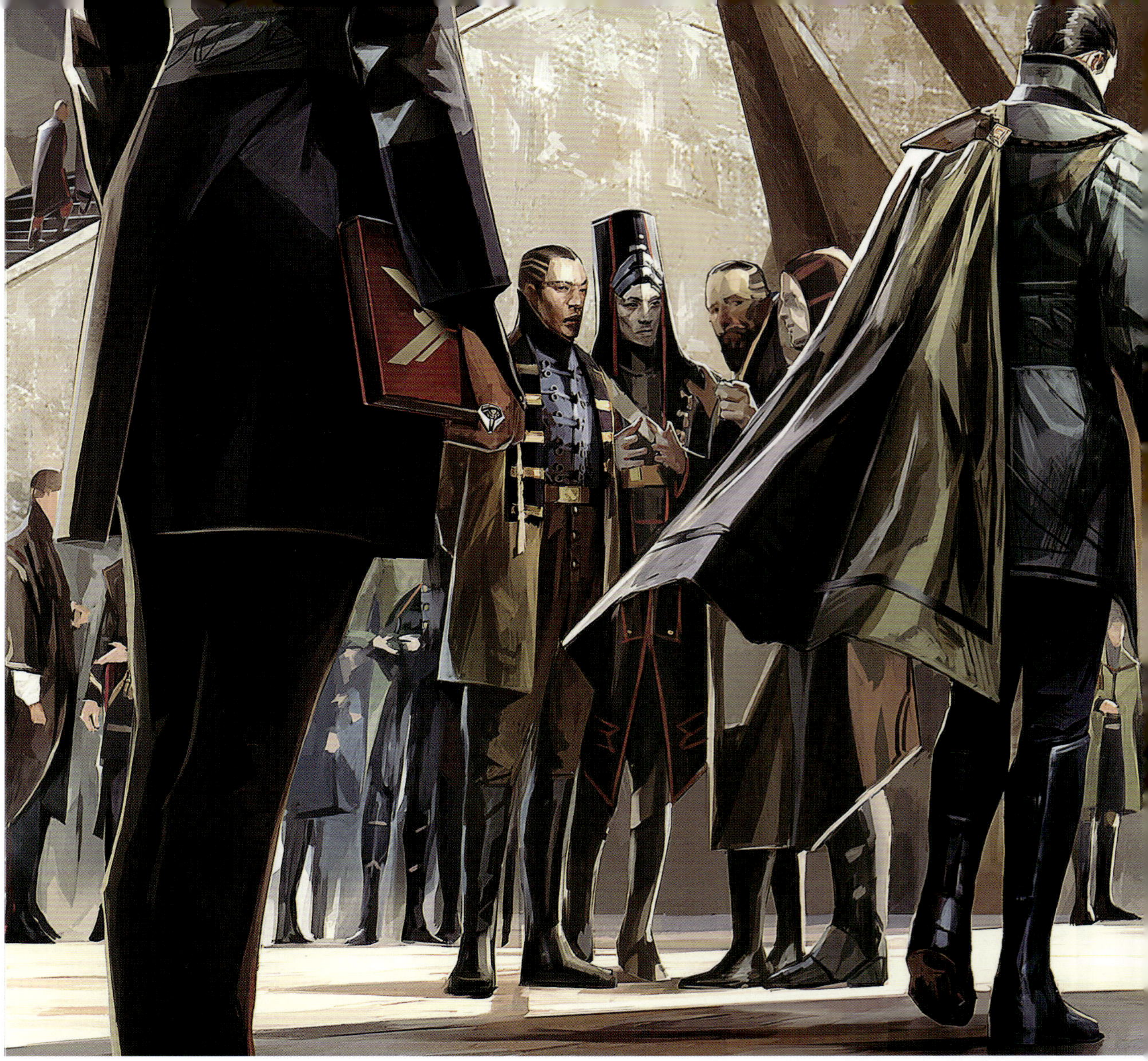

VIEWS
PIECES
CHEST
FRONT
BACK
HELMET
FRONT
LEFT
BACK
GLOVES
FRONT
BACK
BOOTS
FRONT
BACK
PANTS
FRONT
SIDE
BACK

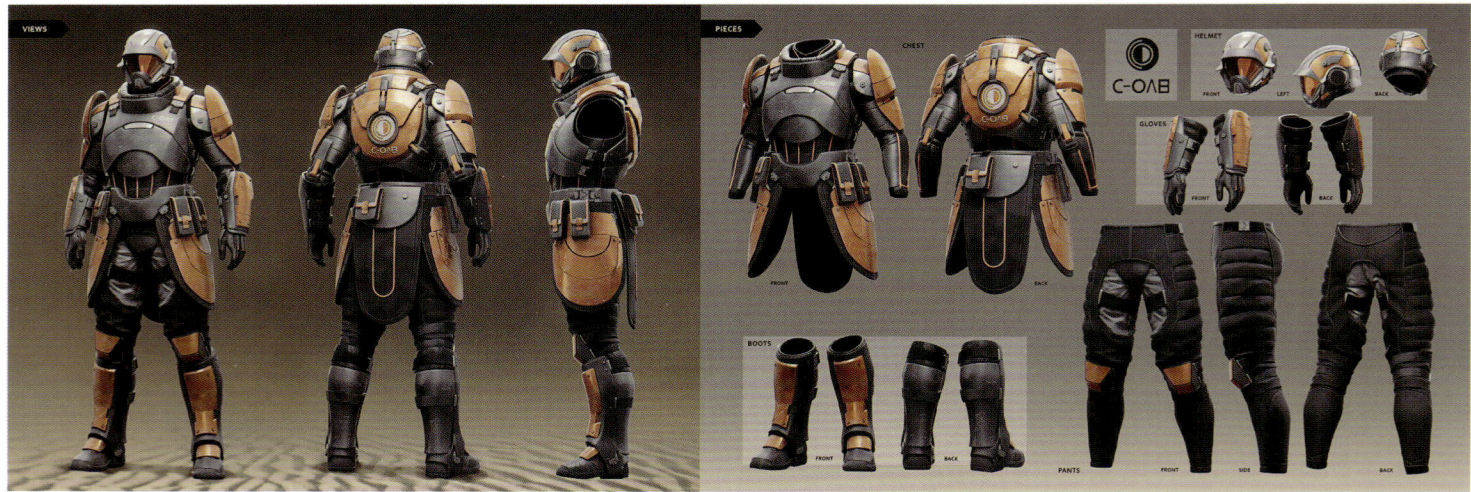

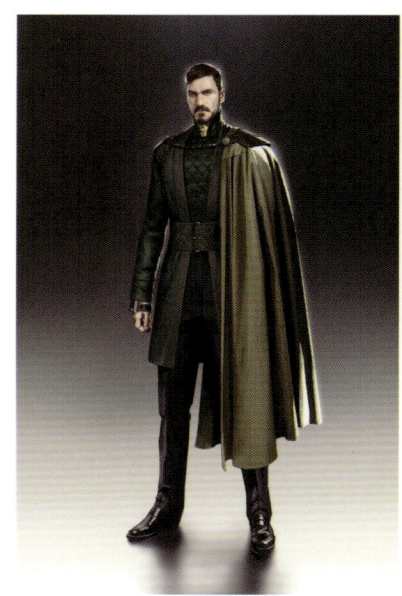

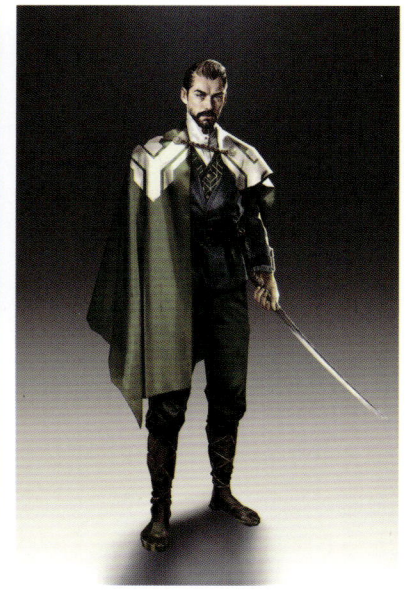

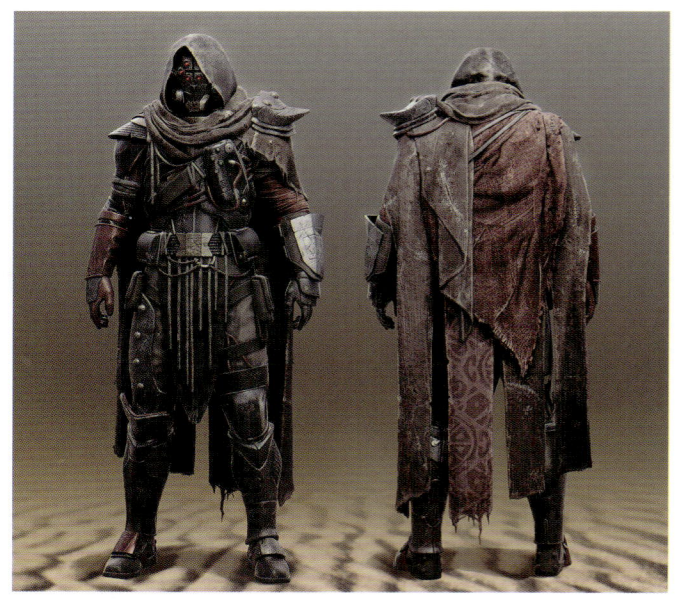

TOP ABOVE *A scene depicting the Harkonnen's ostentatious disregard for water on Arrakis.*

ABOVE *Breakdown of a Harkonnen scout armor set.*

OPPOSITE TOP *Breakdown of a CHOAM heavy armor set.*

OPPOSITE BOTTOM LEFT *Designs for various Atreides uniforms.*

OPPOSITE BOTTOM RIGHT *Designs for a Harkonnen Deserter armor.*

PILLARS OF THE GAME

At the heart of *Dune: Awakening* are four tenants that guided the game development team through their creative journey, ensuring that they would not lose the narrative focus in a bold and complex reimagining of the Dune franchise. "We have four narrative pillars that we follow in the game," says Joel Bylos. "Freedom. Identity. Addiction. Erosion. Freedom, identity, and addiction are all worked upon by erosion. And that's what Arrakis represents. It erodes peoples' character. It changes who they are. When you make characters like Duke Leto, he's a great example, since he didn't die in the Battle of Arrakeen. He wasn't killed, and the betrayal didn't happen because Jessica caught it earlier. Then you have this idea that Arrakis has been eroding who he is. In the movies, he's this noble, well-respected, well-liked leader who's a little bit naive. He thinks just by being good to people, he'll survive.

"In our game, he has survived, but the cost of that survival may have been his ideals. This is the erosion of Arrakis working on him. Maybe this means that over time, his character has had to make painful decisions that he never had to make in the original universe, in the eight-plus years they've been on the planet, at war with the Harkonnen. And that takes its toll on him. And it's the same with the other characters."

The removal of Paul Atreides alters the history of Arrakis in ways that range from subtle to seismic. The Fremen have vanished. Lady Jessica obeyed the Bene Gesserit and gave birth to a daughter, heir to the House Atreides. Duke Leto Atreides survived the assault on Arrakeen and is now locked in a brutal conflict with the Harkonnen over Arrakis and its precious Spice.

This unique but still familiar take on the iconic sci-fi universe of Dune offers a world of infinite possibilities for die-hard Herbert enthusiasts and relative newcomers alike in a multiplayer survival open-world crafting game that allows players to experience Arrakis as never before, whether alone, with friends, in collaboration or competition with hundreds of others as gamers determine their fate on the most dangerous planet in the universe.

OPPOSITE TOP *The First Trial of Aql: "Who is it that keeps the water?"*

OPPOSITE MIDDLE *The Third Trial of Aql: "Who is it that shapes the sand?"*

OPPOSITE BOTTOM *The Fourth Trial of Aql: "Who is it that calls the Maker?"*

ABOVE *Biome exploration depicting the gnarled vegetation of O'odham.*

LEFT *Concept art of the learning center in the O'odham region.*

RIGHT *A meeting with an NPC in the garbage-strewn alleyways of Arrakeen.*

- **SURVIVE** by learning the ways of the Fremen. Seek the shadows to escape the scorching sun. Craft stillsuits and extract water from your enemies to stay hydrated. Build shelter to escape lethal sandstorms, and always beware of the sandworm.

- **EXPLORE** a vast, open world of beauty and danger. Glide, climb, and speed across Arrakis using iconic Dune tech such as ornithopters and suspensor belts. Visit the hubs of Arrakeen and Harko Village, bustling with other players to socialize and trade with.

- **DISCOVER** a shifting desert that offers infinite exploration. Coriolis storms reshape the Deep Desert, turning familiar ground into treacherous, unknown territory. Every week, players race to be the first to uncover new locations, dangers, and rewards.

- **SANDBOX** combat allows you to approach every situation differently using a wide arsenal of ranged and melee weapons, technology, abilities, and even vehicles. From humble beginnings to unthinkable strength, every step fuels your rise to greatness.

- **MASTER** one or all of the Great Schools of the Imperium: Bene Gesserit, Trooper, Mentat, Swordmaster, and Planetologist. Use manipulation and trickery, poison and grenades, dart rifles and cryskives. And remember: the slow blade penetrates the shield.

- **SPICE** is the most valuable resource in the universe. Control, trade, and consume it to unshackle your potential and fuel new powers. Rise from a nameless survivor to ultimately summoning the desert's greatest force: the sandworm Shai-Hulud himself.

- **CREATE** a persona as unique as your ambitions. Craft anything from Fremen stillsuits to Harkonnen ornithopters and fine Atreides furniture. Customize endlessly with emotes, transmog systems, and swatches that let you stand out in the desert.

- **UNCOVER** the truth behind the Fremen's disappearance. As you survive, explore, and build your way to power on Arrakis, you will unravel an engaging storyline unlike anything seen in a multiplayer survival game before.

- **BUILD** anything from a temporary encampment to an impenetrable fortress with a robust, flexible building system. Convert your buildings into blueprints that you can sell to other players on the server-wide Exchange, along with anything you harvest and produce.

- **UNITE** or compete with other survivors—or choose to play alone. *Dune: Awakening* features a highly immersive and persistent online world shared with thousands of other characters and several hundred people playing concurrently. Player versus player (PvP) is always optional.

RIGHT *Sketches of the Waterfat Manor.*

OPPOSITE *The Hand of Khidr is a high-reaching rock formation located in the Jabal Eifrit region.*

PAGES 42-43 LEFT *Concept art depicting radiated craters in the Sheol biome.*

PAGES 42-43 RIGHT *Concept art of the Waterfat Manor.*

Genesis 41

- **GROUP** up with other players to delve into ancient imperial testing stations, collaborate creatively using the robust co-op building system, or simply visit the Arrakeen and Harko Village social hubs to grab a drink or trade on the Exchange.

- **LEAD** or follow, the choice is yours. Join or create a guild, swear allegiance to the Atreides or Harkonnen, and work together to secure their power in the server-wide Landsraad whose decrees impact every player on the server.

- **RISE** to power through the ranks of the Atreides or the Harkonnen. As you build a reputation with your Great House, you will access unique faction rewards such as equipment, vehicles, and building pieces. Ultimately, you can pledge your entire guild to their cause.

- **CONTROL** the Spice, and you control Arrakis. The ever-shifting sands of the Deep Desert offer not only infinite exploration but also infinite rewards. Here, players, guilds, and the Great Houses battle over massive Spice blows to fuel their finances—and their ambitions.

LEFT Concept design of the Harko Village map.

BELOW Exploration of a secret door found in sietch architecture.

REBIRTH

There is another path for you. Awaken. Your new life begins offworld, in the confines of a large spaceship. "It is here in the presence of the Reverend Mother that the character creation begins," says Joel Bylos, Chief Creative Officer of Funcom. You awaken as a nameless prisoner, but now you have the opportunity for a fresh start on Arrakis, the most dangerous planet in the universe."

"This is a place where few people survive. But those that do become the greatest versions of themselves," says Barnaby Legg. "I think that's a great metaphor for the gamer experience, right? We as gamers love to put ourselves to the test, find out what we're capable of. In that way, the planet of Arrakis and the version of Arrakis that Funcom have so brilliantly created really can act as a crucible for the player to find out what they're made of."

The creation process allows you to customize and sculpt your appearance, with an array of physical attributes that allows each player the opportunity to create their own personalized avatar through variables. These variables include age, height, body type, skin tone, hairstyle, and muscle tone, as well as tattoos and other body modifications. "You've had everything stripped away from you. The game begins with not just a traditional character creation screen—we've all been through that, where you get to pick your hair or clothes, all of that—but in *Dune: Awakening*, you must submit to the test of the Gom Jabbar," says Legg. "You must face the Reverend Mother and put your hand in the pain box, and as every Dune fan knows, that is a test of your humanity. To find out if you've got what it takes to survive."

This process, the selection of your character class, abilities, and physical attributes, is folded into the gameplay from the very beginning, setting *Dune: Awakening* apart from the typical SOC. "The character selection in our game is more philosophical than most," Sam Rappaport observes. "This is inherent to how you start the game and the abilities that you get at the beginning of the game. As you go through the process, you think about whether you want to play a character who uses brute force or someone who's more tactical, philosophical, or spiritual. Whichever archetype you want, but it feels very Dune, as you go through the Gom Jabbar test. I feel that it's the best jumping-off point from a character creation perspective. In most other games, that's very separate from the game and you're just dropped into the game right after you decide what your character's going to look like. Ours is directly tied to the gameplay from the very beginning.

"The level of familiarity with the IP allowed us to create an alternate universe that let us play around with the lore without going too completely afar from what's been established in the books and the films, and I think the dedicated Dune fans will appreciate that. We want to keep it as lore-friendly as possible, and there were some major narrative conceits we had to make to do that. But we set up a scenario where you as a player get to live out Paul's fantasy but without him being there. You get to do that yourself. As opposed to another game where you play as Paul Atreides. Here you get to play as yourself and get to interact with many of the familiar characters that you know and love from Dune. I think it just adds that layer of familiarity, but it also let us expand where we needed to, in an organic way."

PAGES 46-47 *Concept art depicting the altar room in the Trials of Aql.*

OPPOSITE *Layout design of the Reverend Mother's pain box room.*

That second stage of character creation will determine your path. "Then I will sift your words for lies," says the Reverend Mother. "Let's begin. Where were you born?" While your hand is placed within the pain box, the Reverend Mother holds at your neck the Gom Jabbar, the high-handed enemy, a poison needle tipped with meta-cyanide used by Bene Gesserit Proctors in their death-alternative test of human awareness. "Don't pull away or you will die," she continues. "Great plots are afoot in the Imperium, and the currents of intrigue run deeply. Arrakis is the key."

Under penalty of death, you decide upon your history, you pledge your allegiance to one of the Great Houses, and your decision will determine your fate. "The second phase of character creation is where you get to make choices about who you were before the game starts," says Joel Bylos. "Where you come from. What caste you belong to in the Dune universe. And of course, perhaps most importantly, who your Mentor was, which determines your skill set when you enter the game."

Those decisions will have a great impact on your mission from the outset. Will you pledge your loyalty to the Imperium and Emperor Shaddam, or does your heart lie with the House Harkonnen or the Landsraad Council? Do you have the spirit of a warrior, as an elite Swordmaster or Trooper, or do you have the mental and physical prowess that aligns with the Mentats and the Bene Gesserit? Or perhaps you see yourself as more of a scholar, an archaeologist or Planetologist driven to learn all that you can about your new homeworld. Your destiny is in your hands. "This was super inspiring for us to see people who were thinking about every aspect of how people move in this universe, how they feel in this universe," says Bylos. "And it's a different kind of approach than we take with video games, and I think it colored our approach when we started working on the game itself. We thought about the characteristics of these people on the movie screen, and how we might mimic that.

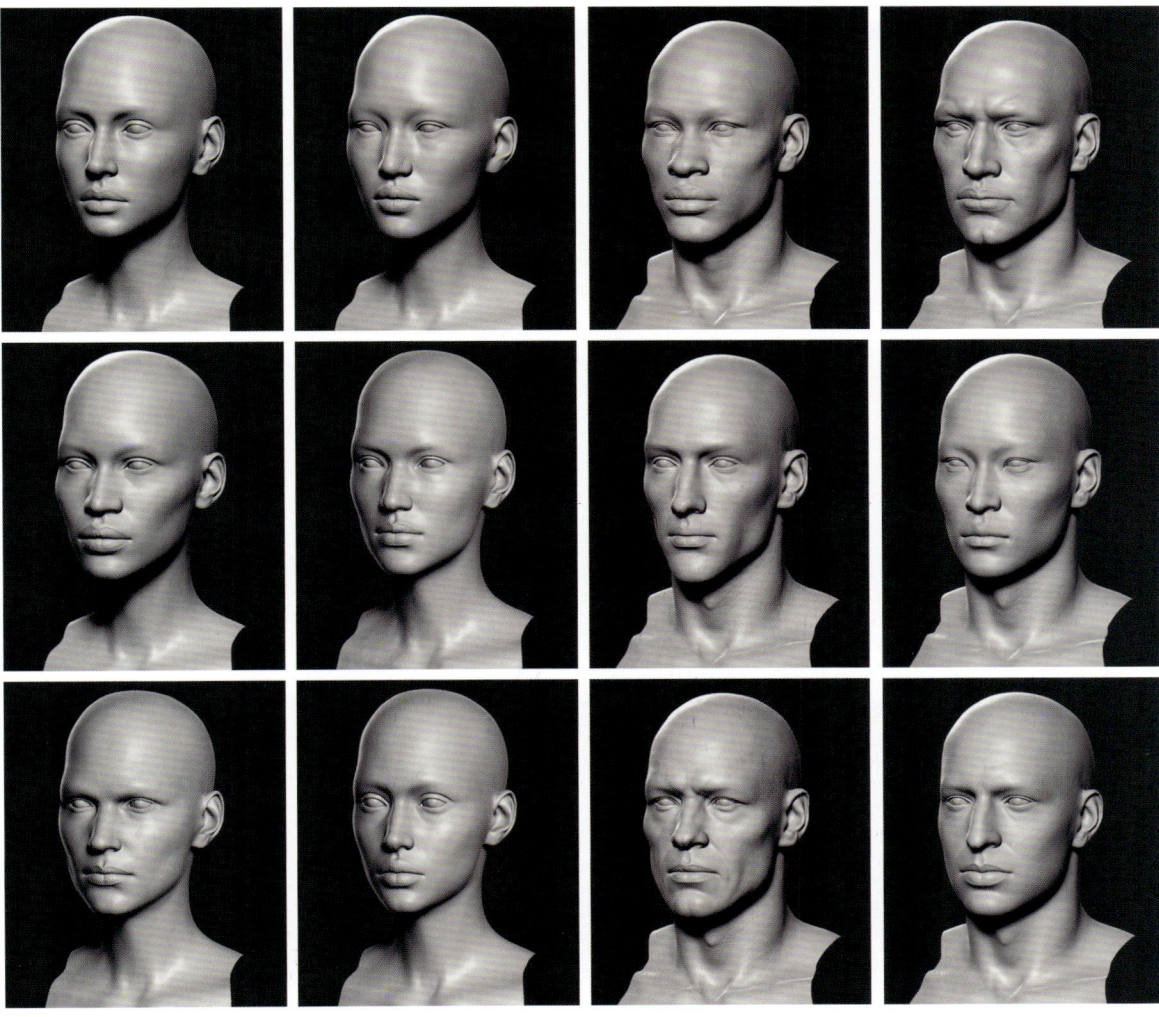

OPPOSITE *Character creation screen showing options for hairstyles.*

ABOVE *Archetype designs for the Kirab bandit faction.*

LEFT *A variety of head sculpt designs available in the customizer.*

Rebirth

"From my perspective, with character creation, there are two ways to do it. In-universe or out-of-universe. A lot of games choose to detach it from the game so that you choose your visual, press the start button, and then you're in the game. And it's sort of disconnected from the game. I didn't want to do that, because I feel there's going to be a lot of people who play our game who don't know anything about Dune. And character creation is a really opportune time to teach them, if they know nothing, but we can also take the people who do know something and give them some familiar elements from the books and the films.

"Right after you choose your appearance, you go into the pain box test, and you make these choices about who you are. If you know nothing about Dune, you can scroll through these options and get an explanation of the different ranks and roles and their place in the hierarchy, as well as an explanation of the strange and thought-provoking Dune terminology that we'll be using throughout the game; I think that makes a more meaningful impact on your character. Then when you get to the actual pain box test, you learn about it here. If you've seen it in the movie, then you recognize this and its importance. We set out to make this the 'Dunest' of the *Dune* games, and you should really feel that."

"You choose an archetype, and that's how you start out," he continues. "But you can actually change that. You can meet trainers throughout the game who can change your archetype, change how you play. It sets your feet on the path into the universe. Another thing that I wanted to do, since this is a space game that takes place on one planet, it's really about this intergalactic, universal game where what happens offworld will impact what happens to you on Arrakis. We needed to make sure the players got a sense that there was more than just the one planet right at the start of the game, because once they start playing, they'll get this myopic view of just Arrakis. But as they progress, the politics starts to come back, and they're reminded of that opening."

The established lore of the Dune universe places inherent limitations on a player's abilities based on their choice of Mentor. "Obviously, in Dune, there are a lot of very memorable and interesting types of characters and orders that you want to be able to emulate and play as a player," says Nils Ryborg. "But it has a lot of strong rules as to what you can and can't do, right? People want the Bene Gesserit abilities, want to be Mentats, Swordmasters, and so on. Now the problem is, you know, only women can be Bene Gesserit, and you need a lifetime of training as well. Same thing with the men that you were raised from a very young age to be a Mentat. And we had to figure out a way to allow people to play into those fantasies while staying true to the Dune lore and to the Dune IP.

OPPOSITE, ABOVE *The five available classes in* Dune: Awakening: *Trooper (opposite top), Bene Gesserit (opposite bottom left), Mentat (opposite bottom right), Planetologist (above left), and Swordmaster (above right).*

BELOW *Early explorations of the starting tutorial shipwreck vista.*

OPPOSITE *Concept art of a shipwreck crashed down in Arrakis.*

"We made a very specific decision, which is that the player and every player on Arrakis is going to be a Ghola, a creation made by the Bene Tleilax [an order made up of genetically altered humans whose biological experiments and questionable ethics have earned them the enmity of the rest of the known universe]. In more simple terminology, we would call it a clone, but it's not exactly that. They have kind of taken your DNA and created you as a person again. You have everything except your memories. This is a big part of the plot line in the second and third Dune books, as the Bene Tleilax's goal for immortality is to find a way to awaken the genetic memory within their Ghola, thus achieving immortality. Because as they get old and frail, they can create a new version of themselves. The old person dies, but the new person lives on, and you can live on forever, right?"

Once you have passed the test of the Gom Jabbar, you are given a new lease on life and the Reverend Mother designates you for assignment on the planet below, where your destiny awaits. "The Fremen are missing. You will go to Arrakis as our agent, Prisoner. You have one task. Find the Fremen. Wake the Sleeper. You will know when it is done."

With your new identity in place, you set course for Arrakis. A crash landing leaves you abandoned and alone, with no resources at your disposal, in a desperate bid for survival. The harsh and unforgiving sun and sand, deadly creatures lurking just below the surface, enemies hidden in every shadow.

Welcome to Arrakis, the most dangerous planet in the universe.

"You start with nothing. You are stranded in the middle of the desert, and you have to figure out what your water source is going to be. Then you have to find some basic clothing, and you have to figure out how to fight basic characters, and you peel back these layers as you discover abilities and explore the world further and further," says Sam Rappaport. "We wanted to make sure that the landscape didn't feel like one giant desert, so Funcom explored all of these different biomes that were very inherent to Dune but feel different enough where, as a player, you're going to see enough variation that you'll want to explore each of these different landscapes. These other regions will still feel very dry, very true to the world of Dune, with sandy Arrakis vibes, but in a different way."

The truth behind your mission, and your very existence, will be revealed over the course of a long, treacherous journey. "Who is the player? What's going on? Why are we here?" asks Nils Ryborg. "These are all the questions that we want to kind of put into the player's head at the start of the game.

"You are a nobody at the start of the game. You don't know what's going on. We've set the stage. You don't know who you are. You are taken in. You're tested by what appears to be a Reverend Mother. You discover what your background is, who you think you are. People think this is a character creation where you get to create who your character was. It is not.

"This is a conditioning check. They're making sure the implanted memories you have are in fact there. You're sent off to Arrakis with the goal of finding the Fremen and waking the Sleeper. This is all very vague, and it is meant to be quite vague. And as you're going down to Arrakis, your plane, or the ship, rather, gets shot down by a mysterious hooded figure. You get pulled out of the wreckage and the figure somehow seems to recognize you, spares your life. And here you get through to your little tutorial area, the person who saved you and shot you down, both sides of one coin."

THE ROAD NOT TAKEN

ABOVE *Renders of Ariste Atreides's head and fabric patterns.*

OPPOSITE *Full-body design iterations of Feyd-Rautha Harkonnen (top two rows) and Ariste Atreides (bottom two rows).*

The world of *Dune: Awakening* will be very familiar to those well-versed in the Dune mythos . . . but also dramatically different due to the absence of Paul Atreides. The loss of Muad'Dib, the Kwisatz Haderach, has changed the lives of all who had known him in the original timeline, especially those closest to him and his family.

"We see everyone in a different story setting," says Sam Rappaport, "and see how their lives have changed in this alternate timeline. We get characters like Duncan Idaho in *Dune Awakening*, for example, still serving Leto Atreides, even though he dies midway through the original novel. Being able to explore all those characters without the need of navigating the film side and the books was very interesting. Gurney Halleck is no longer driven by his need to avenge Leto Atreides but is still driven to protect the House Atreides. The actions of characters, including Lady Jessica, Wellington Yueh, Stilgar of the Fremen, and the Harkonnens, all change because Paul was never born."

The ramifications of Duke Leto's survival and all the alternate decisions and branches of the timeline that occur as a result have altered the political landscape of Arrakis in ways large and small, according to Dune lore expert Joel Bylos. "Duncan Idaho is loyal to Leto Atreides, but what's going on with the Duke is making him question things. Jessica and the Duke have more of a wedge between them because she bore him a daughter instead of a son and chose her loyalty to the Bene Gesserit over her loyalty to her Duke. That created a rift in their relationship.

"Then you have Ariste, the daughter, who has a different set of pressures on her than Paul ever had. The daughter of the House of Atreides is supposed to marry one of the Harkonnen, Feyd-Rautha Harkonnen in our case, to give birth to the Kwisatz Haderach. In our timeline, there's a different kind of pressure from the Bene Gesserit on all these characters. It's an interesting dynamic for sure. For people who have read the books, it's a different path to explore.

"Gurney Halleck's sister was killed by the Harkonnen when he was young, so he still doesn't like the Harkonnen, regardless. He's always anti-Harkonnen. When you meet him in the game, it's clear that he's very protective of Ariste. And very set on preventing the Bene Gesserit from having their way with the wedding that they want to occur."

RIGHT *Concept art of Count Fenring.*

BELOW *Character style for a Bene Gesserit sister.*

OPPOSITE TOP *Further Bene Gesserit character explorations.*

OPPOSITE BOTTOM *Atmospheric art depicting a corridor inside the hidden sietch.*

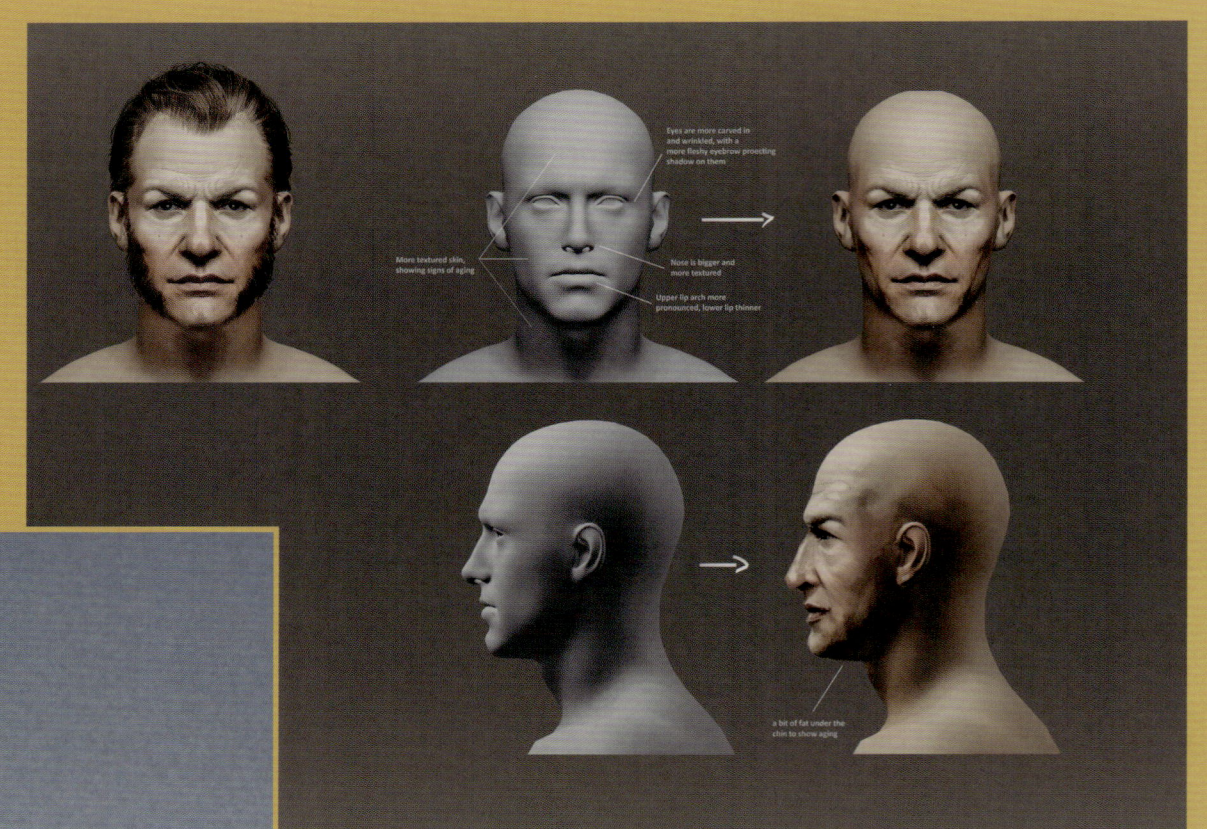

Paul's absence has also altered the fate of his adopted tribe, the Fremen, as their prophesied Messiah never traveled to Arrakis to take his place as their leader, their chosen one. "We went as deep as the lore would allow us to, in terms of Fremen culture, with what the game mechanics would allow," says Rappaport. "A lot of that was putting things like traversal into the game, making that feel good and engaging as you learned how to traverse the desert in a fun and interesting way. You're learning and trying to develop your character as a Fremen, but you're also trying to determine where the Fremen are. In the beginning of the story, the Fremen are mysteriously missing, so you're getting your information from things like cave drawings and people who are aware of the Fremen who are giving you advice along the way. We wanted a journey of exploration."

The decisions that you made immediately after your awakening will determine the course of your journey. Hidden memories and training buried within your subconscious will allow you to access the abilities that not only will help you to survive Arrakis, but as with Paul Atreides himself, will grant you the potential to become one of its great leaders. "Thanks to your pre-awakening conditioning, you have received all these trainings that you need in order to be able to access the abilities of the Kwisatz Haderach from the start," says Nils Ryborg. "Now, obviously players won't know this and they'll consider this a bit of a plot hole when they start the game. But as the reveals come in later on, they'll be able to see that this was a plan from the very beginning, all part of the Bene Gesserit plan to protect the House of Atreides. They need the daughter of Lady Jessica to survive because her child is going to be the Kwisatz Haderach that they've been awaiting for millennia.

"Meaning that the House of Atreides survived the attack on Arrakeen, meaning Duke Leto is still alive. So are Lady Jessica and all the other big-name characters that died off in the movies and in the books. In the storyline, the emperor blames the Harkonnen for the attack and has given them the right to have a war of assassins down on Arrakis.

"The story of *Dune: Awakening* unfolds about fifteen years after the events of the first book. And there's been a long war of assassins between the Atreides and the Harkonnen. We're setting the stage here for the player to come in and interact with the world where all the big-name characters are still available. They're around; you get to interact with them. That's very important to us as fans, and it gives us plenty of space to navigate with the story."

Helping you navigate your new world are a Fremen warlord called Zantara and Bronso Vernius, from the Brian Herbert novels, a noble offworlder who, like Paul Atreides, has journeyed to Arrakis to join the Fremen. Through your encounters with Bronso Vernius, the Bene Tleilax hope that you will awaken your memory and unleash your full potential. "You have little time to escape from the wreckage of your ship," says Ryborg. "The Sardaukar are coming down to rescue some of the ship's crew, and you are not included. You're going to get killed if you stick around. You escape, you come out to Arrakis proper, and now you get into the survival gameplay loop.

"The story you've been left with is you must find the Fremen, but you don't really know how. In the first part of the game, you're just trying to survive. As you spend some time on Arrakis, as you ingest the Spice that is just naturally on the planet, you will at some point pass out and you will have what we call a Spice Dream. It's a weird, trippy kind of horror-y moment where a person that you do not know yet who is Paul Atreides speaks to you from a different timeline in the form of a Muad'Dib, and he gives you a hint as to how to find the Fremen."

The fate of the Fremen is one of the most important mysteries of *Dune: Awakening*. Every political faction on Arrakis is determined to uncover the truth behind their disappearance, including a stranger who may very well become your greatest ally as you strive to complete your mission . . . or your greatest foe. "Zantara is this mysterious figure who picks you out of this shipwreck at the start of the game," says Joel Bylos. "He's actually the one who shoots down the ship. But there's something he recognizes about your character that makes him not kill you. Because he's killing all the other survivors of the crash, walking through the wreckage and killing people. But he recognizes you, stops, and saves you. He helps you and offers advice throughout the game and is a bit of a mentor to your character. But as the story unfolds, you find that he is one of the main terrorists wanted by the Imperium. One of the last Fremen freedom fighters, since the Imperium claims that they've killed them all. Stilgar is still MIA. Nobody knows where he is in the game. Zantara is the only link to the Fremen, but he claims that he is not a Fremen himself.

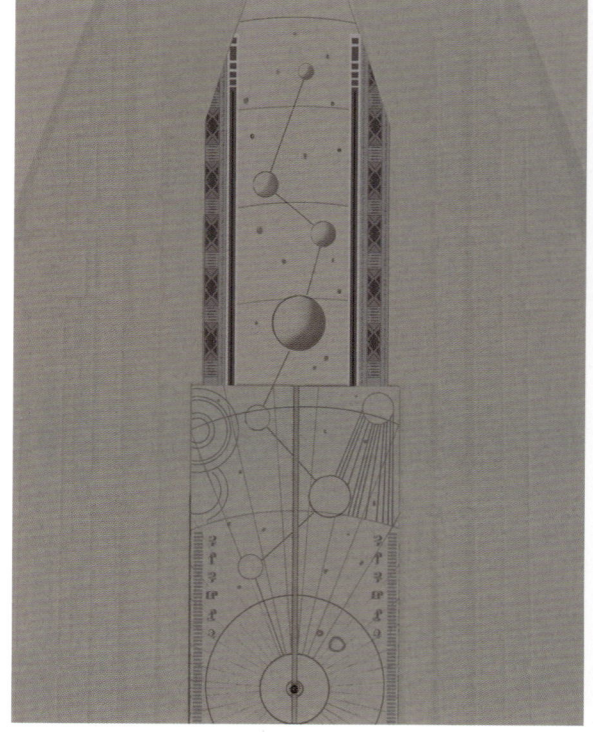

TOP *Concept art of the hidden sietch antechamber.*
BOTTOM LEFT *Sketch of the antechamber star door.*
BOTTOM RIGHT *Render of the Deathstill.*

"As you explore the game, you learn that Zantara definitely has contact with the Fremen and that there's more going on here than meets the eye with his character. He's hell-bent on revenge against the Imperium. He takes a stand and does some of the things in our game that Paul Atreides did in the movie and the novel. Not because he's the Kwisatz Haderach, but because some of those same actions need to occur. Paul nukes the shield wall to get to Arrakeen when the emperor's there, while Zantara nukes the shield wall to let sandworms into the basins to make it harder for the Imperium to carry out some of their operations.

"There are some parallel events that occur in our timeline caused by Zantara, so it creates an interesting juxtaposition."

Despite these unfamiliar faces and storylines, many elements familiar to those who know the Dune mythology will guide them through their journey. "You must take the Trials of Aql," says Ryborg. "These are tests that the Fremen children do to become fully fledged adults, and so the player is now spending the part of their gameplay going around looking for different locations of these trials and completing them. Some they can do, some they cannot.

"Some have been destroyed by the Sardaukar and their pogrom against the Fremen. And throughout all of them, you're picking up little clues about the journey the Fremen went through before they came to Arrakis. This all culminates in you finding a hidden sietch. It's been abandoned, but you don't know this yet. You make your way just inside, and you are accosted by another hooded figure. This is a Fremen scholar who calls herself Ari. In time, you will discover that she hides an incredible secret, one that will change the entire course of your journey. But for now, she's just a scholar who will help you investigate this, the sietch.

"In the sietch, you find your first real clue to the Sleeper and the Fremen. A hologram recording left by a person who doesn't really refer to themselves as anything specific. The internal name is 'Agent X,' but this person is the Sleeper that you're looking for. He somehow knew that you were coming here, because the hologram recording that he left indicates that only your blood would let you into the specific chamber.

"We're trying to build again here the mystery of, who are you really? Why do you keep showing up in all these different locations? Why do people seem to know you?"

OPPOSITE *Explorations for Fremen armor design.*
ABOVE *Render of the Deathstill puzzle.*

THE WORLD OF ARRAKIS

SAND FLIES

Few planets in science fiction are more dangerous than Arrakis. Its unforgiving environment, from the intense heat and sudden, violent sandstorms, proves fatal to unprotected humans. Extreme conditions ensure that only the strong will survive.

"The biggest challenge was taking the lore of Dune and converting it into a world that you actually get to experience and play without breaking the rules established by the original novels," observes Sam Rappaport. "It's one of the most important sci-fi properties, and we didn't want to make a game just for the sake of making a game. We wanted to give people the opportunity to explore Arrakis themselves in a way that they couldn't really get in the context of a feature film or television episode.

"[We're] really riding this line of having a game heavily inspired by the vision of Denis and his creative team while giving Funcom the creative freedom to explore other characters and equipment that aren't seen in the films—elements from the book that weren't developed by the filmmakers—and they put together these big lore pieces that were true to the world, as they had to extrapolate these into the actual game mechanics."

The geography of Arrakis is an essential part of that lore, which players will discover as they explore the dunes and uncover the secrets hidden beneath the desert sand. Among these is the sietch, a cave warren inhabited by a Fremen tribal community; or, in the Fremen language, "a place of assembly in time of danger."

PAGES 64-65 *Hagga Rift visual exploration.*

OPPOSITE TOP *A megafactory in the Vermilius Gap region.*

OPPOSITE MIDDLE *Imperial testing station interior.*

OPPOSITE BOTTOM *Bandit bases architecture style exploration.*

TOP, ABOVE *Biological imperial testing stations.*

OPPOSITE *Geological imperial testing stations.*

PAGES 70-71 *Huge-scale space port visuals.*

To bring these iconic Dune elements to life, the game developers worked in lockstep with the production team from Denis Villeneuve's films to ensure their vision of Arrakis would complement the visual identity established by Patrice Vermette and his team. To accomplish this, the creative departments from Legendary and Funcom would have to take a long, difficult journey to a world unlike their native lands of Los Angeles and Oslo, but fortunately for them, much closer than Arrakis. "Our game has been

in development since the first movie was officially greenlit, many, many years ago at this point," recalls James Ngo. "The game was a high priority for Legendary, and everyone involved wanted us to have access to all of the resources that we would need to make this not just a successful adaptation of the world established in the films, but something that would both complement that world and also stand on its own.

"When the first movie was being shot in Budapest, I was able to take a team of Funcom people, the creative director, the CEO, the artists, to do a tour of the set. It was very inspirational for us to see the movie at that stage, to share in Denis's vision. It was such an emotional, educational experience, and it really energized the entire team as we commenced production on Dune: Awakening. Games take five, six, seven years to make, so I wanted to get us all on the same page together from the outset. We really started when they started on the first film in 2016 and have been charting our course together."

The set visit provided the creative team with an inside look at everything that the art department and production team had planned for their *Dune* movies, which ensured that the work of the *Dune: Awakening* team would draw from the same sources and the visual language established by the filmmakers. Though not beholden to the movie, Funcom and Legendary realized that with an official *Dune* game would come certain expectations in terms of fidelity to its source material. "I feel the most important aspect of that set visit was that we really got a sense of the look of the first film very early on in our development process," says Sam Rappaport, "but in addition to that, we were able to fully appreciate the scale of everything that Denis was creating. It was truly awe-inspiring.

"In addition to Patrice Vermette, we met with the costume designers, Robert Morgan and Jacqueline West, as well as fight coordinator Roger Yuan so that we could be in lockstep creatively with the films. It's one thing to share concept sketches and production art over a computer screen, but it's another thing to be on location and gain firsthand knowledge of the production, as the look and the feel of the films really inspired our team to take things to the next level."

TOP *Concept art of an Arrakeen courtyard.*
ABOVE *Environmental art of Harko Village.*
OPPOSITE *Concept art of the Harko Village spire.*

SET PIECES

The summit between Funcom and Legendary Entertainment on location in Budapest marked a turning point not just in the production of *Dune: Awakening*, but for the members of the creative team as well. "I'd never been to a movie set before, so I didn't know what to expect. We arrived in Budapest, and it's got those old, Eastern European, communist Bloc buildings on the outskirts, but it's a beautiful city in so many ways," says Joel Bylos of Funcom. "We came into downtown, then we took a bus out to where the set was. Very high security, which makes sense, since it's such a big, big-budget production, with a lot of money behind it and a lot of creative partners involved. We went with our representatives from Legendary and got to visit the different sets. I think the thing that struck me the most in that first visit was the scale, and the attention to detail, which I wasn't expecting, because there's a lot of CGI these days, to be able to walk around inside the Arrakeen palace that had been built by Denis's team."

Although many of the Legendary Entertainment team members had visited movie sets in the past, none of them witnessed a production the size and scale of Denis Villeneuve's *Dune*. "It was an incredible experience across the board. It was one of the first times that I met any of the folks at Funcom and the people actually designing the game," says Sam Rappaport of Legendary. "It was neat to support the development in this way and to take them to the set.

"What was really cool for me, since I'm still kind of a nerdy kid who loves video games and Dune, is that I'm still coming at it from more of a fan perspective. It was really incredible to share that experience with everybody.

"When we got to set, it's probably one of the few movies that's built physically at this scale. You walk onto the landing pad on Arrakis where they first open up the shuttle doors and you see the ornithopters—all of that was built out, physically. We also got to see the Arrakeen palace, the insides of that. They really just built out the entire thing. The scale of it is spectacular. It was an awe-inspiring experience for everybody, and it really sets in the gravity of what the filmmakers are trying to create, and what the production crew has done. That was very beneficial for the games team, because you can read scripts, you can look at things on your computer screen, you can see concept art and set photography, but when you really get to walk around and see the size and scale of everything, how it looks in person, the scale of it all . . . that's incredibly helpful from a game developer's perspective."

TOP *Exterior of an Arrakeen landing pad.*
ABOVE *Interior of the landing pad.*

"Seeing the ornithopter up close and knowing how many people can fit inside, how many seats are inside and how they're arranged, how to arrange the control consoles as well," says Rappaport. "To see the kind of future tech that comes from an analog place, because there are no thinking machines or AI. Patrice Vermette did a wonderful job of riding those two lines, where nothing ever looked too techy, or too filled with lights and meters and things. It looked very analog, almost like a World War II airplane."

In a notable departure from contemporary sci-fi and fantasy productions, nearly everything on the set was built out, with the filmmakers opting to create physical sets, props, and vehicles whenever possible. "First of all, it was mind-boggling that so many of the buildings were built of Styrofoam," marvels Bylos. "Because it looked like sandstone. I don't know how they would have built a set like this in the past, but it was just beautiful up close. I think we saw rooms from Caladan, the rooms that they'd built, including the round window where the rain is pouring, sitting in that shape.

"We got to see the military ornithopter and the Planetologist ornithopter, obviously very different styles. It was incredible to see them from afar, but then to study them up close, to actually sit inside . . . that was very cool."

ABOVE *View from the upper floor of an Arrakeen bar.*

OPPOSITE TOP *View from an Arrakeen landing pad.*

OPPOSITE BOTTOM *The interior of an Atreides building.*

The World of Arrakis

And thanks to movie magic, Bylos and his team were able to study the iconic weapons and artifacts of Dune, things that they had only seen in earlier live-action adaptations of *Dune* or had only read about in the original novels. "We were able to visit the prop department and see all of the little details they were adding, like the crysknives and the swords and the kindjals. It was really interesting to talk to the creatives there to find out what they thought about Dune. About the Harkonnen, who were beastly and brutal, and the shape of their swords reflected that, while the Atreides are more elegant and more civilized, so they have a more rapier-style dueling weapon," he continues. "And the Sardaukar as the elite troops have a slightly different saw-toothed weapon. It's very interesting to see how much thought they put into the detail. Not just the lore of the books, but the thought they put into the visual storytelling in the movie, like how much someone, at a glance, would be able to read into these things, and we discussed how that would be transferrable to the game.

"And then we went to watch the stunt team training, which was really interesting. We spoke with Roger Yuan, who was also acting in the films, and they were showing us how they approached the different combat styles. How the Harkonnen would use treachery, and that was part of their built-in combat. One guy would always go behind the other person fighting, kind of hiding so they could push them over the top or stab them on the ground. There was no honor to the way they fought. Whereas the Atreides fought in this much more honorable way, with a one-on-one approach. And the Fremen, they have this motion of rising up, like coming up from the sand, which is like a metaphor for their entire people throughout the movie. Rising up from under the sand to take out their enemies."

The Legendary and Funcom teams were given full access to every aspect of the production to ensure synchronicity and visual continuity between *Dune* and *Dune: Awakening*. The opportunity to walk, live, and breathe Arrakis was an invaluable educational experience for the game development team. "Another highlight was when we met with Patrice and he took us around the art studio where they do all the concept art, and we talked to him about his art and his inspirations," says Sam Rappaport. "Same with the costume designer and the fight choreographer and the armorer. All of that stuff is physical, so you can pick weapons up and get a sense of how light or heavy they are, how big they are, how intricate those things are. The fight choreographer walked us through his inspiration, and we drew from that when we developed the game. We weren't trying to make the game a one-to-one adaptation of the movie, but it had to feel like it was part of the same universe while living outside of it.

"And with the costumes, seeing them, feeling the fabric and talking to the costume designer about her influences and inspirations, seeing how the different fabrics flow on the mannequins and the people, seeing how intricate or how simple things were. You can look endlessly at set photography and concept art, but when you can really see it and feel it, it gives you an incredible sense of the love and attention that goes into everything. It's inspirational to get that sense that we're all on the same team, creating this universe together. And they're letting us behind closed doors to see what they're doing.

"If there was ever a movie set to visit, this is the one," Rappaport continues. "Because they built everything out. There was so much physicality to everything. We may have seen one green screen the entire time we were there. All of the interior shots, Paul in his bedroom, the scene where Paul does the Gom Jabbar test, all of that was built out. You get a lot of personality from the physicality that you don't get from a room with a cool-looking carpet and a green screen around it. You live and breathe Dune, and it's much better for translating the gravitas of that into a game."

OPPOSITE TOP *An Arrakeen entrance hall.*
OPPOSITE MIDDLE *A scrap store located in the Arrakeen market.*
OPPOSITE BOTTOM *A hologram displayed in the market hall.*

Members of both productions, the filmmakers and the game developers, bonded over their creative aspirations and love of all things Dune no matter their background, country of origin, or role in the production. "Definitely quite an experience," says Rappaport. "There was a lot of fun and anticipation building up to the visit. You're preparing to meet these people working on a big Hollywood film, and you don't know what they're going to be like, what headspace they'll be in; you just know that you're meeting with all these people.

"But the coolest thing about it is that everyone is just a person. Everyone is super nice and willing to talk and to have conversations about what's inspirational to them, and how they got to where they were and how they came about thinking about all of this stuff relating to Dune. It's nice to feel that love and attention from everyone who's working on the films. There were no egos to anyone. They were excited to talk to people about the thing they love doing the best. They smile, and they're happy to talk you through everything. Everyone is working toward the same thing, and they're all excited about the project. No attitude. Just a big happy family making this cool dream project."

OPPOSITE TOP *Render of an Atreides LMG.*

OPPOSITE BOTTOM *Renders of an improvised Maula pistol (top) and a Sardaukar sword (bottom).*

BELOW *A vehicle store located in the Arrakeen market.*

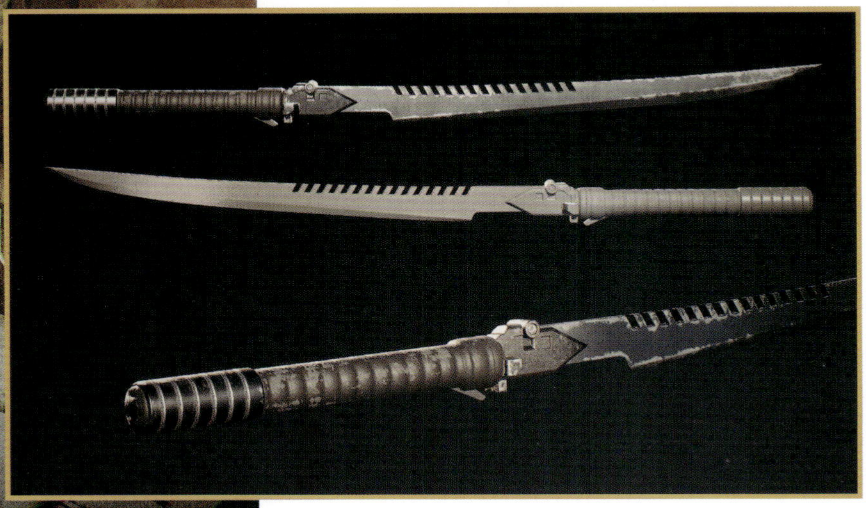

The World of Arrakis

81

THE ROAD NOT TAKEN

"After we visited the set, we went back to Oslo with Funcom to have a planning session to determine what the game would be, the rough story points that we want to attack. And that's how we landed upon setting this in an alternate universe," says James Ngo. "There are certain things that work very well for literary purposes, certain things that work very well for cinematic purposes, and certain things that work very well for game purposes, but they don't always align with each other. This was a great way to give Funcom the expressive liberty that they needed to play with all of the different storyline elements that they wanted while not having to follow the exact story of the films as well. This allowed them to explore other aspects of the world of Arrakis, life there, whether or not we saw them in the films."

The exploration of those other aspects allowed Funcom and Legendary to chart terrain, regions, and even cities that went largely unexplored in the films, granting them a creative freedom that was both very liberating and very intimidating at the same time. "It was a real challenge to the game developer team," says Barnaby Legg. "Arrakis is this beautiful, exotic world, but it is, of course, very barren. Endless, infinite deserts where little can survive, or even thrive, and one of the things that video game worlds really thrive on is variety. Not always feeling like you're in the same environment, that you have a lot of different ecosystems to explore, so that the world you're exploring doesn't feel too 'one-note.' Funcom did a brilliant job of bringing a real diversity to the environment.

"It's not just the Deep Desert where Shai-Hulud awaits. It's the hidden depths that lie beneath the surface as well. The hidden temples. The lost civilizations. And it's also, critically, about the world that you the player can architect. You can build your own vast locations that are an expression of who you are and your creativity. At first glance, the world of *Dune* and *Dune: Awakening* may seem like this infinite open horizon of desert, but I'm really excited to see players turn it into their own Arrakis with their own unique features and landscapes."

TOP *Large-scale industrial remains within Vermillius Gap.*

LEFT *Concept art depicting caves in the Vermilius Gap.*

Those landscapes include several player hubs, cities where players can meet, exchange resources and information, congregate, and form alliances. One of the first regions that players can explore once they progress from land to air travel is the southern port known as Harko Village. "The village is the current seat of the Harkonnen after their city Carthag was destroyed in a nuclear explosion during the War of Assassins. There are more details like that in the lore of the game for players to discover and explore," notes Funcom Chief Creative Officer Joel Bylos. "Once you arrive in Harko Village, you'll be able to meet up with other players, interact with them, trade, and create guilds. The game has a variety of social interaction mechanics from emotes to grouping to a chat. Throughout Harko Village, you'll also interact with story characters. Follow the main story. You'll be able to meet vendors who will sell you exotic items. You will be able to get a sense of how the factions are viewed in the world, and of course you'll be able to swear allegiance to one of the major factions, the Harkonnen or the Atreides. Swear your guild's allegiance and begin to take part in the politics of the Imperium."

The War of Assassins is one of the major repercussions of the ripple effect caused by the nonexistence of Paul Atreides, the Kwisatz Haderach, as you will discover over the course of your journey. "Heading out into the world can be a dangerous experience, and as you explore the universe, you'll find certain dynamic events will occur," says Bylos. "In one such case, the War of Assassins has claimed a new victim. A ship falls from the sky, spilling its loot all over the sand, so we head over there to see what we can harvest and gather as much as we can. Of course, the problem is this is extremely visible to everybody in the nearby area, so people will be able to see this. In a PvP area, you might suddenly find yourself coming into competition with other players to get to the loot first.

"Of course, at nighttime, there are different kinds of threats because the heat of the day isn't as dangerous as night falls. The Sardaukar patrol this area of the desert with huge spotlights, searching for players. Now this player is over here harvesting dew with a dew reaper sucking the water off the surface of these plants, but now they've been seen and captured by the Sardaukar, and they come floating down out of the sky to attack and destroy the players."

OPPOSITE *A Harko Village building.*

TOP *The back entrance to Harko Village.*

ABOVE *Render of a Harko Village main street.*

RIGHT *Harko Village Spice vendor.*

The World of Arrakis

As you explore, the history of the region unfolds and reveals itself to you. Clues from NPCs and holographic messages will guide you through the overland map to destinations, including Old Carthag, a city devastated by a nuclear explosion that is now populated by strange creatures that have adapted to a climate that is somehow even harsher and more uninhabitable than Arrakis in general. Information obtained in Old Carthag leads to Hagga Basin South and into the Vermilius Gap, which lead to Jabali Fritz and the Hagga Rift. "You can kind of go between the two of them and can move up to the shield wall or move on to the Udem region and then finally on to the shale, with different factions inhabiting each region," observes Nils Ryborg. "We picked the Hagga Basin as a location for a reason. It's got a good kind of location vis-à-vis Arrakeen and so on.

TOP LEFT Concept art of a Harko Village vendor stall.

TOP RIGHT Harko village entrance checkpoint station.

RIGHT Harko village vendor street stalls.

The World of Arrakis

"But then we had a couple of decisions we had to make. For instance, Carthag, which was the city built by the Harkonnen, and their kind of seat of power on Arrakis, is really close to Arrakeen. It was a logistical problem for us, right? As part of our alternate history, we had that city nuked, and they're building Neo Carthag a bit further away. This is, you know, part of the story. Ironically, on the surface, the storyline is that it was destroyed by a kind of rogue mining issue, some ultimate tech going haywire," Ryborg continues. "The truth is it was Fenring who blew it up because there was a Ghola lab under Carthag and he has to stop the Ghola because of the whole usurping-the-emperor plot, which is why we end up going there at the end of *Act Two*."

The game developers were fairly locked in when it came to the development of locales such as Arrakeen, which were featured prominently in Denis Villeneuve's films, but the alternate timeline caused by the destruction of Carthag allowed the creative team to explore the architecture, politics, and society of Arrakis in a state of transition. "Arrakeen is obviously iconic, and because of its place in the films, we tried our best to reproduce that," says Joel Bylos. "But because our game takes place in this alternate timeline, we tried to imagine how that would change in this different scenario. This place that was attacked but managed to survive. How is it different now that this city isn't broken down, isn't war-torn? In the books, the Harkonnen have this capital called Carthag. In our storyline, Carthag got nuked by an accident, so they've been forced to live in this little village called Harko Village while they're rebuilding their capital, which they call Neo Carthag. There's a sense that they've been displaced from their great city. Off in the distance, you can see Neo Carthag being built. Neo Carthag, meanwhile, is very cramped. Very brutal. They have a lot of slaves around as they're trying to rebuild their original city. That was very much setting up a contrast for players, so they'll say, 'this is Dune, but it's not the Dune I've read about.'"

OPPOSITE *Various interior angles of the Imperial Consulate in Harko.*

ABOVE *Concept art of the Harko Village imperial consulate exterior.*

POLITICAL FACTIONS

The alternate history of *Dune: Awakening* allowed Funcom the freedom to reinvent the map of Arrakis, even though many die-hard fans of the novels—Ryborg among them—will know that some creative license was required to accommodate all the player hubs that would be necessary for gameplay. "We had to make some adjustments to Neo Carthag, particularly its location, since that is under construction at the time of *Dune: Awakening*," notes Ryborg. "We have the Hagga Basin kind of in the middle, in a perfect location. But then in the Hagga Basin, we kind of had to create that locale, and establish its history and its inhabitants. So there are multiple factions in here that are our own creations that fit within the universe, but they're not explicitly named in the books.

"We have the scavengers going around scavenging, trying to make sense of things, because there's been the big War of Assassins, meaning a lot of ships and vehicles and things have gotten destroyed. So that's how they're surviving. We also have a faction called the Kirab, which are a kind of banded faction, praying on the scavengers. You've got slavers again, praying on everybody, and they're selling most of their slave labor to Neo Carthag construction.

"We've got the Sandflies, which is a kind of revolutionary organization made up of former Spice miners trying to get a better deal," Ryborg continues. "But they're also kind of semi working as bandits. You've got a bit of a 'freedom fighters' situation in that they're kind of good in a way but also kind of bad in another way. Some people consider them terrorists; some people consider them liberators. You can kind of go either way. And then as part of the whole thing, we've got the Mascarats, which are a cult started by Fremen wannabes."

ABOVE LEFT *Harkonnen wall decorations.*

ABOVE RIGHT *A Harkonnen building.*

RIGHT *The interior of a Harkonnen building.*

The World of Arrakis

ABOVE, RIGHT *Atreides player building set interiors.*

OPPOSITE *Landscape scene showcasing the architecture of Mysa Tarill.*

The apparent disappearance of the Fremen, the most notable tribe on Arrakis, has disrupted their entire region as other factions attempt to fill the void that has been created by their absence. "The Fremen are gone in our story so far. They pulled back to the Deep Desert, but people think they're dead," says Ryborg. "And so these people are trying to inhabit their place, but they're just a wannabe cult ironically created by one of the player's 'siblings,' who, instead of finding the Fremen, created their own that you have to fight your way through. We spent a lot of time developing these groups, discussing the political factions, and talking through these developments, because each addition and each subtraction would create its own very real story problems. This was necessary on our part because some of these aspects were mentioned only briefly, or sometimes not at all, in the *Dune* novels.

"They focus much on the kind of high-level political stuff. But we have to deal with people on a day-to-day basis, right? So getting into the books is great and will help you a lot, but there's also a lot of stuff going on in our game that is unique to us that we have to deal with.

"With the Mascarat, for example, we made the decision to reuse armor styles from previous factions because these are people who defected from who they used to be to join the Mascarat," Ryborg continues. "The Mascarat are a group that is very physical, 'of matter.' Like, for them, it's a texture matter. Like, they've got other outfits and then they're using different textures and then they've got some unique helmets to give them a little bit more identity. But like, they're purposefully reusing other people's armor, for instance, to symbolize that they are not their own thing. They're just an amalgamation of weirdos, basically."

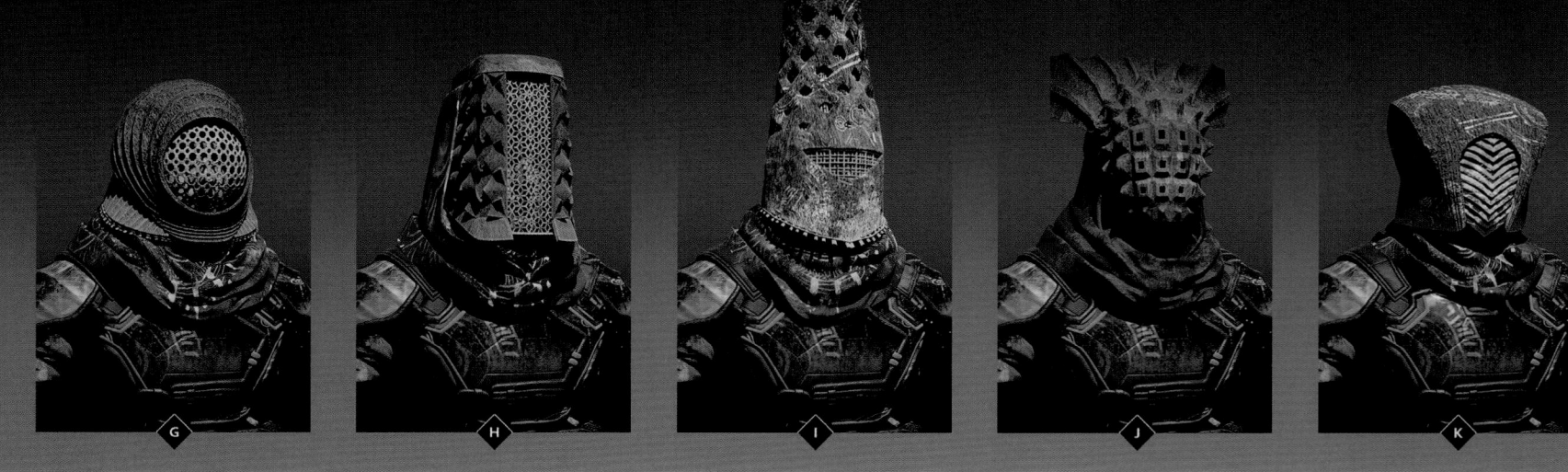

And that "amalgamation of weirdos" adds to the tapestry of *Dune: Awakening* to create a truly immersive Arrakis unlike anything that gamers could have ever imagined, including those who were involved in its creation. "I think there's something, particularly in a post–*Dark Souls* world, where gamers are really excited about a true challenge, really being pushed to the limits. There's something exciting about being presented with a world where even just the weather can kill you," says Barnaby Legg. "They're looking for a level of challenge and a level of intensity. If you want to go someplace where you'll have to test yourself and push yourself to the limits just to survive, in all of popular culture, it's Arrakis. The definitive place where humanity doesn't belong.

"The level of immersion that video games can bring is so unique. And here you're teaming up with other players, collaborating with other players, forming alliances, making enemies. The fact that people can experience Arrakis and take that journey together allows for some unique storytelling. Stories where the players themselves are the authors. You can walk your own path and build your own story alongside your friends. You can experience the story in an unusually social way. And this is a planet where very few will survive alone. You really do need to get a bunch of friends together and make the trip to Arrakis together, and you'll get a lot more out of it."

Members of these different factions will cross paths throughout the various player hubs scattered throughout Arrakis, from major cities to isolated outposts found in the desert sands. "I think what's really nice about the cities and player hubs is that it gives you a whole new way to experience Arrakis," says Sam Rappaport. "There's a lot of stuff that's not

ABOVE *Iterations of Maas Kharet assault gear.*

OPPOSITE TOP *Ceiling of the Mysa Tarill boss room.*

OPPOSITE BOTTOM *The Mysa Tarill gate.*

necessarily unanswered, but in the films, you don't get to spend time with the inhabitants of the cities, to see what the people are doing, seeing the day-to-day existence, the commerce, the activity. It's an extra layer that we have, exploring the corners that you don't get to see in the films or the TV series. That's important to us as the IP holder, since we don't want to just make a game version of the films. It's meant to support the franchise in a bigger way. To have those Easter eggs and cool areas of the map that are more or less glossed over because they don't have anything to do with the linear storyline of the movie."

TOP LEFT *Maas Kharet Pyon ruins.*
TOP RIGHT *Maas Kharet character concept.*
OPPOSITE *Maas Kharet meditation chamber.*
ABOVE *Renders of a marksman helmet.*

The World of Arrakis

FOUNDATION

Arrakis's reputation as the most dangerous planet in the universe is well-documented. The daytime heat is intense. Basic natural resources, including shelter, food, and even water, are scarce. The landscape is inhospitable. The deadliest creatures alive live below the surface. Natives find themselves in a constant state of war with the world around them just to survive, and transplants learn immediately that the dunes will test them in ways they never could have imagined before their arrival on Arrakis.

One of the keys to survival is learning that on Arrakis, nothing is wasted. Every resource from the largest ship to the smallest droplet of moisture is precious, and those who can control those resources and master their environment will survive—and even thrive—on an unforgiving world. "One of the coolest things about this game is that, unlike other survival games, there's really something for everyone," says Sam Rappaport. "When you reach the endgame and you go to the Deep Desert, all of that is PvP style where you have to protect yourself, and you're always looking out for other players as you're jamming into these Spice Flows to get as much Spice as possible, but if you're more of a solo player and you want to just explore and be on your own, you can do that as well. You can do everything from being someone who just wants to mine resources or, if that's not your interest, you can go to someone who is doing that and just buy resources from them. And you can scale that up through the entire economy. If I want to be a weapons dealer, I can build up my arsenal and you can purchase weapons from me."

Another key aspect of survival is your ability to salvage resources from abandoned ships and structures, which will allow you to craft your own tools, weapons, vehicles, and bases, which in turn will help you remake the landscape of Arrakis to suit your needs and to fulfill your objectives. The fabrication process allows you to build anything you can imagine, from a basic shed to a literal fortress, depending on your architectural needs and inclinations. "Building bases is a big part of the game as well," says Rappaport. "If I'm someone who just wants to build cool things, like a LEGO-style expert, I can build things and save those blueprints and sell those blueprints to other players. It's a very good mix of multiplayer and single-player experience, and you can even change your approach from day to day if you want to do that.

"In addition to traditional base building, we've added design elements from the original lore as well as the films. Glowglobes and other items can be used to decorate your buildings. You can start with a very small, basic building, but as you progress throughout the game, you'll encounter people who have built five- or ten-story megabases. You can set different levels of security, too, so a solo player will be the only one who has access to their buildings and vehicles, but in team play, you may want your entire guild to have access to those resources. It gets pretty elaborate.

"You don't want it to feel samey. You don't want a vast landscape that's nothing but sand and rocks. Where you start is very basic—beige-toned desert, a vast empty landscape—but as you progress, there's a red sand desert, then you progress to caverns and cliffs that you can explore on your ornithopter, hundreds and thousands of feet deep, with shipwrecks and imperial testing stations, which are like underground dungeons. There's greenery and other elements that provide a very

different environment. One area is slightly more populated with flora, and exploring those things makes the world feel a lot bigger than the vast open desert."

As you and others collect resources and gain experience, you will have the opportunity to stake your claim and reshape the very world around you. "After you've played the game for a little while, you'll want to build your own base," says Joel Bylos. "The first part of that is placing what we call a Sub-Thief Console, which allows you to claim a small part of Arrakis as your own. But it does in turn mean that you'll start to owe taxes to the emperor, so players must be aware of that. The building system utilizes holograms, which allow for a cooperative building system. One player places projections while the other fills them out with materials from their inventory, which lets them play together and build together.

"We've created a blueprint building system that allows players to save a copy of their base as one of these giant holographics, then they can take them out into the world and place them wherever they like. You can also sell them to other players on the Exchange. It also allows you to quickly rebuild elsewhere in the world. If you're not artistically minded, you can buy bases from other players."

PAGES 98-99 *Nighttime at the Red Desert megafactory in the Vermilius Gap.*

TOP *Vista over Hagga Basin South.*

ABOVE *Concept art exploration of how Spice appears in the game and interacts with the landscape.*

Foundation 101

TOP *A jail-themed building set.*

ABOVE *CHOAM shelter set building interior.*

OPPOSITE *Harkonnen-style floodlights.*

That flexibility and the collaborative nature of the game allow players the ability to shape Arrakis and the potential to remake the world—and perhaps the entire universe—as they imagine it. "The genre that we've done most of in the past is the survival genre, where you have a lot of building—you build your base in the world that's your sort of space. And we wanted to bring that to Dune," says Bylos. "The idea is that people build these very bunker-like buildings in the beginning to avoid the heat of the sun, staying on the rock islands to avoid the sandworms. Very simple, very practical.

And we wanted people to have a lot of flexibility in that building system. The potential to create beautiful things, even though they're just using concrete slabs to build. But as you progress and join a faction, you get access to the kind of buildings they would have. For example, the Harkonnen buildings are very [H. R.] Giger-esque. Very dark. Broody. Faces in the architecture reminiscent of organic shapes within the doorways. Whereas the Atreides structures tend to be more like a palace or a castle. Futuristic. It's not just about the players expressing themselves creatively but also about expressing their identity based upon who they've aligned with in this conflict.

"Free-form building is not new, but allowing people to do it in this large, open world is a real challenge. A lot of work for us."

And a lot of work for players as well, but fortunately, that task is aided by Arrakeen technology straight out of Frank

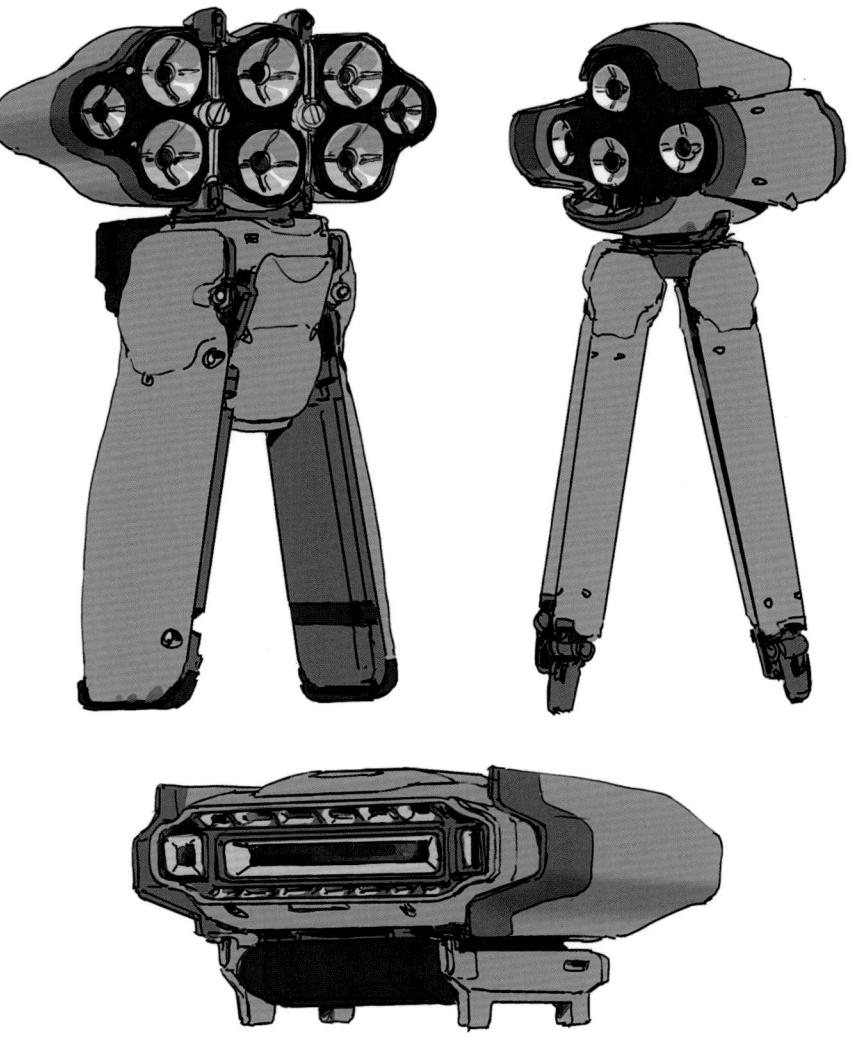

Herbert's original novels. "The movies use sand compactors, or static compactors—it's called both in the book, but we call it a static compactor. That's a cool and really interesting tool. We tried to find all of the things that only exist in Dune and focused on those in the game to make a truly unique player experience that doesn't feel like anything else," says Bylos.

A fortified, safe base, whether it's a simple, utilitarian cube or a more complex structure, is essential to your survival and your ability to traverse and explore Arrakis beyond whatever terrain you can cover on foot, racing from one shady outcropping to the next. "Once you finish crafting a base, you want to fill it with all kinds of machines, fabricators, and refineries. And machines like the Blood Purifier, which can refine blood that you've collected into lovely fresh water, which can be carried into the desert," Bylos continues. The ability to manage your own level of hydration and vitality opens up greater opportunities for exploration as you encounter structures, including wrecked spacecraft, abandoned buildings, and laboratories such as the mysterious desert testing stations. "Once you've grouped up with friends, you should go out into the world and find desert imperial testing stations," says Bylos. "These are dungeon-like experiences that you and your friends can work through together. For example, we can land our various ornithopters outside of one of the desert testing stations. We can head in as a group. Then it's really important to prepare different skills and abilities. These areas tend to be more of a challenge, and it's great to work together to complement each other.

"As you progress, you'll add more talents to the onscreen skill tree. You can equip different types of abilities and techniques. We have three slots for abilities and three slots for techniques, and there are multiple different trees depending on the type of trainers that you've interacted with in the world, which will allow you to equip a series of abilities that complement the rest of their group, such as Swordmaster techniques. The stations have storylines as well as enemies to fight and loot to be found, so you really want to go there and enjoy the experience playing through with friends, working together, using different weapons, and trying out different techniques. When you get to the end of these areas, you find these really cool loot chests, where you can find specialized components that are used for crafting exotic weapons and items."

ARCHITECTURE OF ARRAKIS

Players have the ability to craft their own buildings to suit their own sensibilities and in-game needs, but a team of architects, designers, and technicians studied with the production team on the *Dune* films to ensure that their vision of Arrakis complemented that of Denis Villeneuve and Patrice Vermette, building a world that feels like a natural extension of the cinematic universe. "There are things you can do in movies regarding architecture. For example, like in Dune, it's Arrakeen. Hard angles, simple shapes. The brutalism," says Morgan Sandbæk, Associate Technical Director at Funcom. "That presented us with a real challenge in terms of finding interesting things to set up in the game world. When you're making a film, you survey the landscape, you set the stage, you set the camera angle, you plan the shots, and you direct what the viewer sees."

That variety results in a game experience unique to *Dune: Awakening*, where the architectural details from the smallest structures to the largest cities reflect the players' sensibilities, according to Legendary Entertainment's Sam Rappaport. "In a game, you want every faction to be very identifiable, because you're giving visual cues to players to go to or to avoid certain areas. As a gameplay mechanic, it's really important to have those cues. And you as a player get to build those different sets and building types that you can interact with, so it's not just standard-looking brick houses that you make while you're exploring the map and seeing all of these elaborate structures that you can't interact with. Here, thanks to the blueprint system, you've got a much more hands-on, ground-up interaction with the world around you.

OPPOSITE TOP *The exterior of an Atreides building set.*

OPPOSITE MIDDLE *The interior of an Atreides building set.*

OPPOSITE BOTTOM *An Atreides table.*

LEFT *An assortment of Atreides decorations, including vases and books.*

ABOVE, OPPOSITE *An assortment of Atreides decorations and furniture available in building sets.*

"Atreides structures are brutalist, while the Harkonnen style is very industrial. It adds a layer as you bring your own perspective and vision to the game. If you're aligned with one of those factions and you and your friends build out a giant base or compound, you're getting into that visual cue. If I'm part of another group or another faction and I come across these compounds that look vastly different than mine, I know that I need to be very careful because I may not be welcome here. It's a lot of fun, getting to customize that yourself."

That customization is one of the most intriguing aspects of the game, says Morgan Sandbæk. "For me, it's about what you can do as a player. You can make a footprint on Arrakis as you build your own base. You decide. You can decide to play with others, of course, and make a guild and do some large-scale changes that will affect other players, but it's the combat challenges that we have and that you need to continuously evolve," he continues. "You can play around with the abilities, different places, craft different play styles. I'm really looking forward to the base building and the PvP, and in the end after reaching the max level.

A: More compatible with classical Caladan furniture style

B: More compatible with Modern Arrakeen Atreides architecture (buildin Set) Clean and Wings Shapes

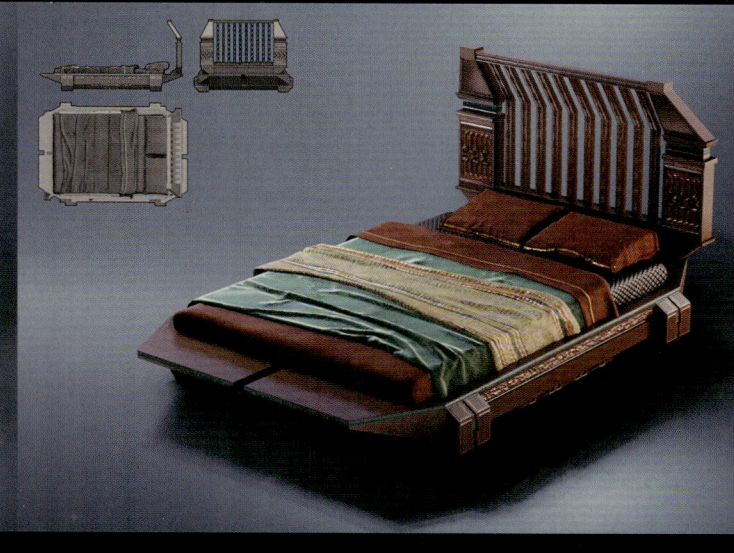

ATREIDES PLACEABLES - Bed and bedding

ATREIDES PLACEABLES - Closet / Wardrobe

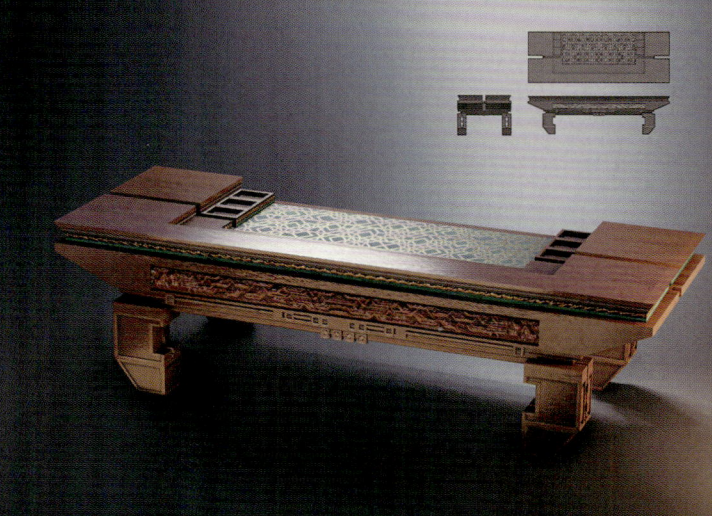

ATREIDES PLACEABLES - Desk

ATREIDES PLACEABLES - Drawer / Side Unit

ABOVE *The interior of a Harkonnen building set.*

TOP RIGHT *The exterior of a Harkonnen building set.*

BOTTOM *An assortment of Harkonnen decorations (left) and furniture (right) available in building sets.*

"When you're translating that to the game world, you need to take into account that what the players can do, and where they can look, that means that they can do anything and look at anything from any angle. That adds an extra layer of complexity, I would say. But that's where you need to play with secondary and tertiary elements and the next layer of detail just like you need. You need layering, basically, to have something interesting. If not, everything becomes flat, and that's been an ongoing effort to land on.

"But I think they're nailing it now, and we know some of the challenges so we can work with them instead of just head-butting them all the time," Sandbæk continues. "Thanks to our creative partners like David Levy, the lead artist on our post-lighting team, doing all the right things to build an interesting environment, while Joel Bylos, our loremaster, as the creative director on the project, lets us know if we're straying too far from what's been established in the novels and the official Dune canon. If he detects something that doesn't feel 'Dune,' he'll let you know.

ABOVE *An assortment of Harkonnen decorations and furniture available in building sets.*

OPPOSITE *An assortment of Harkonnen decorations, including light and wall fixtures.*

Foundation 111

OPPOSITE *Exterior and interior of a CHOAM building set.*
ABOVE *Various stages of CHOAM building sets.*

"But then we have the movies, which also inspire us because they already tried to translate the books into what it would look like in the modern production. And of course, we started on the game a long time before the first movie came out. Not that long a time, really, but still a fair amount of time before the film's release, when most of the team only had seen some still images and the movie trailers. Some had been to the physical set, though, so when the movie first came out, we sort of saw a lot of similarities. There were things that we hadn't seen yet in the movie that we had [to] take a stab at, and it was in the same ballpark. But then they also, in the movie, I think they use the location as a reference, so they even filmed there. At that location we use, we are heavily inspired by the environment in the movies. The real-world sort of reference that they chose. Some exceptional visuals drawn from the movies. That gave us a lot of pointers to where we should look and what we should look at and what we might also adapt for our own use in the game."

Foundation

David Levy, Associate Art Director at Funcom, had worked on the television series *Dune: Prophecy* prior to joining the *Dune: Awakening* team, ensuring a visual continuity between both adaptations. "Our team had to create the social hubs, and we made sure the continuity between what we call the battle areas of the game was integrated with other areas, like the cities," says Levy. "We spent a lot of time studying the architecture of the movie, the way they assembled cities, and we tried to imagine how it would feel to walk through those cities. In Dune, you need to protect yourself from the sun, and logically that means those cities need to be enclaved and offer shelter and shade.

"Walls that would protect people from sand. Shielded. Using the movie as our base, we asked what the streets in the city would look like. To guide us, we looked at cities in the warmest regions of Africa, like Algeria, regions that had an Arabic look and feel to them. We looked at the multilevel towns and villages with stairs and platforms, tents and tarps to create shade.

OPPOSITE TOP *An assortment of CHOAM decorations and furniture available in building sets.*

OPPOSITE MIDDLE, BOTTOM *An assortment of CHOAM decorations, including light fixtures, vases, and book cartridges.*

BELOW *CHOAM books take the form of cartridges.*

PAGES 116-117 *Concept art for the inside of Hannivar's Bar in Harko Village.*

OPPOSITE TOP *A sandbike vendor stall in Harko Village.*

OPPOSITE MIDDLE *A blockade set up in the streets of Arrakeen.*

OPPOSITE BOTTOM *A shuttered vendor stall in Arrakeen.*

ABOVE *An ornithopter vendor stall in Harko Village.*

"In the movie, you see the cities from above, from an ornithopter's views, so you don't really see what it is like to live there. That was tons of fun for us, to create a real, living city, inhabited by real people on a daily basis. The buildings have back doors, the shops are neat and organized up front but have crates and messes in the back and behind the shop, customers come and go. Messy and disorganized.

"Our objective was to make sure that these cities were believable and lived-in, and I feel that we accomplished that."

Foundation 119

THE SPICE OF LIFE

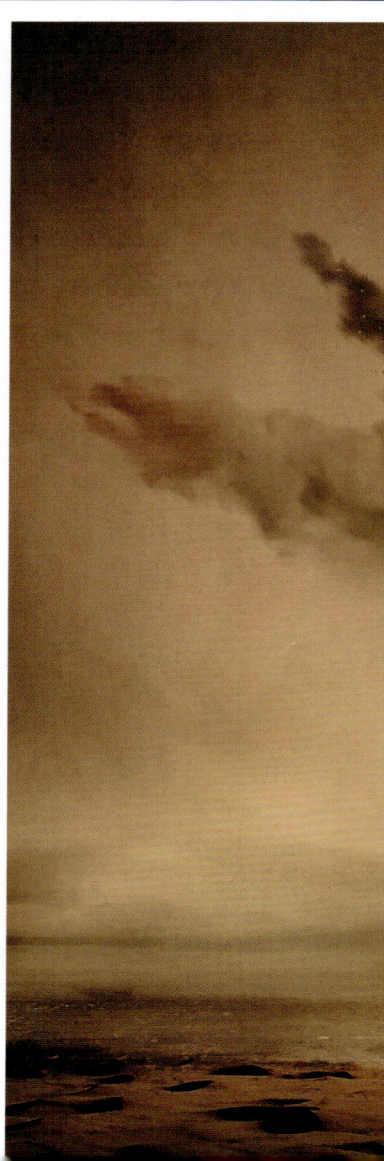

ABOVE *Environmental exploration of a Spice field.*

RIGHT *Concept art of a Spice mask, a piece of gear that filters out airborne Spice particles.*

OPPOSITE *Environmental art depicting a Spice Blow, an explosion of Spice in the Arrakis desert.*

 The Spice of Life

Despite its inhospitable climate and inability to support human life without technological assistance, Arrakis is one of the most important and hotly contested planets in the universe due to its unique natural resources, Melange foremost among them. Colloquially known as "the Spice," Melange is a highly addictive drug essential to space travel, extended life, and therefore the survival of the universe. The most coveted element in the known universe, Spice is Arrakis. Spice is life.

"Spice is central to Dune's lore, and that's true of the game as well," says Sam Rappaport. "There are a lot of Spice-infused items and consumables in the game. Your Spice level goes up or down depending on how much you've ingested and, if you're around a Spice Flow, how close you are to those things. You will also have Spice visions, something cool and trippy that isn't explored too directly in the films, but it's something that we wanted to explore in the game. That was also a way for us to give clues that will help the player find their path through the story. It's true to the lore, fun for the players, and very interactive.

"Spice is part of the economy, too, and is very much part of the endgame. Once you've gone through all of the missions and reach the endgame scenario, you arrive at the open desert and open up all these Spice Flows. You and your friends can basically group up, and if you've chosen that path where your goal is leadership of Arrakis, then you will want to rule the Spice trade.

"You want to, in your server, have the best equipment and go to these Spice Flows in the Deep Desert and mine for Spice. Meanwhile, there are other players who want to do the same thing, and who are trying to keep you away from the Spice, who will plant thumpers when you approach so that they can summon sandworms so that you'll have to get in and out very quickly before they destroy your entire operation. It very much is inherent to the game."

PAGES 120-121, OPPOSITE *Concept art exploring how the team went about making Spice visible in the desert of Arrakis.*

RIGHT *A variety of Spice consumables. In order from top to bottom: Spiced coffee, Spiced liquor, Spiced food, Spiced wine, Spiced water, Spiced beer.*

ABOVE *Environmental exploration of a Spice field.*

RIGHT *Concept art of a Spice mask, a piece of gear that filters out airborne Spice particles.*

OPPOSITE *Environmental art depicting a Spice Blow, an explosion of Spice in the Arrakis desert.*

The Spice of Life

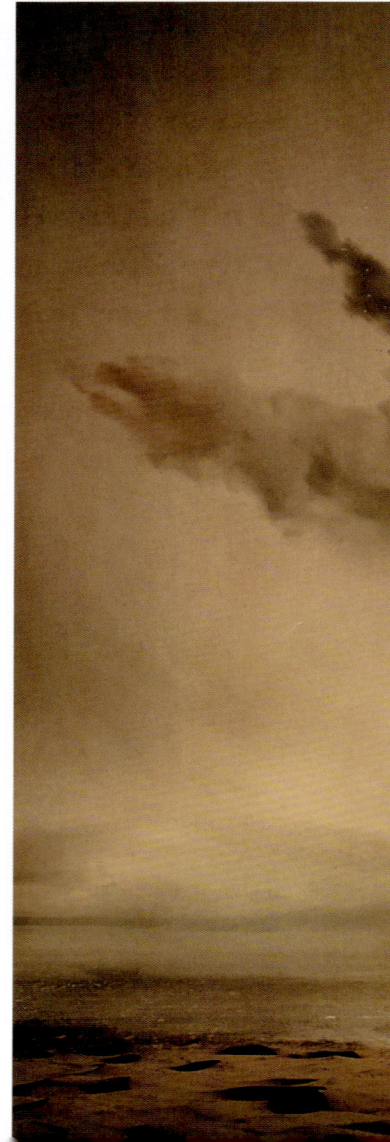

TOP *Environmental exploration of a Spice field.*

BOTTOM *Concept art of an ornithopter navigating a Spice Blow.*

SPICE HUNT

Spice drives the economy on Arrakis, or, more accurately, *is* the economy on Arrakis. "He who controls the Spice controls the universe," said Baron Vladimir Harkonnen, an accurate assessment of the power and influence of Melange over the known universe. Spice is power, and unsurprisingly, people will risk everything to obtain it, braving intense desert heat and sandstorms, the threat of certain death from the sandworms who are inextricably connected to Melange, and the powerful, ground-shaking Spice Blows that periodically erupt and reverberate for miles around.

"The endgame of *Dune: Awakening* takes place in the Deep Desert," explains Joel Bylos. Giant Spice Blows will happen, drawing players from all around to try and harvest the Spice as quickly as possible. You'll want to get there first to take as much Spice as you can before an enemy guild shows up to try to take it from you. Of course, if you're clever and you start to lose the battle, you might place out a thumper, and that limits the time in which people are able to take Spice, because then the big worm is going to show up."

Cultivating the Spice uncovered by the cataclysmic Spice Blows requires bravery, cunning, expert timing, and teamwork . . . and a little bit of luck, too, according to Morgan Sandbæk. "When the Spice Blows happen, you're running around and you sort of hear a sound and the screen shakes a bit and a shock wave comes over you, and then you're sort of looking around and then you see plumes of smoke rising up and then it sort of hits you. 'Oh sh*t, that was a Spice Blow!'"

TOP LEFT *Render of a CHOAM Spice refinery.*

TOP RIGHT *Storyboard laying out the progression of a Spice Blow.*

BOTTOM *Spice Blows create a dangerous environment for the player to navigate.*

Spice Bloom & fields storyboards

- Spice bloom explosion
  - Giant spice bloom cloud visible from a long distance away, several rock islands atleast.
  - Rock debris thrown into air and crash down
  - 2 km shockwave radius both in air and on ground

1a 1b 1c

- Spice fields
  - Spice sand powder radiating outward in patterns around the space bloom explosion site.

2a 2b 2c

- Spice fields - Crater
  - Spice bloom crater. A "donut" displacement around the radius.
  - Should'nt be very steep so there won't be a problem driving down into it.
  - Could have sections around the donut displaced less so there are some easy "paths" down into it.
  - Chunks of rock landed and scattered around the crater with consentrated chunks of spice, and spoky spice steam cloud emitting from them.

3a 3b 3c

- Spice bloom cloud stays in air above crater for a long time after the explosion.

4a 4b

The Spice of Life

Spice Field Crater Rocks

130　　The Spice of Life

"These towers of smoke appear in the environment, and you know that there are valuable resources down there, so you need to go there and get the stuff before anyone else picks it up. So that creates a nice tension when you're in that endgame loop where you're sort of farming for Spice. And the FX team has done a really good job on crafting that big explosion because, yes, we're a game and we can't do what Hollywood VFX simulations need to be.

"It needs to be like runtime experience. And it needs to be massive, and it needs to really, you know, it needs to pay respect to Dune. We went through so many iterations there to get the smoke to look the correct way—the colors of the Spice—and then you get a crater in the landscape after the Spice Blow. And just to have all of the pieces working together, that resources are spawned, and they get the crater and the nice Spice Blow effect and the shock wave. It's quite a system in its own right, and it's more than just [what] immediately meets the eye."

TOP *Renders of a CHOAM Spice refinery..*

BOTTOM LEFT *Chunks of rock produced by Spice Blows, often found in craters after an explosion.*

BOTTOM RIGHT *A crater in a Spice field, created by a Spice Blow explosion.*

The Spice Blows, and Spice itself, have a connection to the sandworms, which—like the desperate people living on the surface—are drawn to the natural phenomena of Spice Blows, as well as any disturbance on the surface of Arrakis, from the smallest footstep to the largest explosion. The risk is great, but so are the rewards. Melange captured from the Spice Blows can be used as currency at the marketplaces in the social hubs, and for those who dare to utilize the Spice themselves, to unlock their hidden abilities, they may unlock the secrets of the universe.

"Spice is at the heart of everything, of the entire universe, for so many reasons," says Barnaby Legg. "With its ability to manipulate space and time and expand human consciousness, expand longevity, expand human life. It is, of course, also the ultimate financial treasure that drives the economy of this world. And I think Funcom did a great job reflecting all those aspects of Spice.

"Spice is essential to the in-game economy and the way you're going to build your character up, to fuel your efforts in your rise to power," Legg continues. "But we also embrace the trippier side of the Spice Melange: to change your consciousness and give in to visions of the future. From the beginning, Funcom wanted to embrace the almost psychedelic aspects of Dune as well. The Spice vision sequences in the game get pretty trippy, and I think players are going to get a real kick out of it."

TOP LEFT, OPPOSITE BOTTOM *An Atreides medium ornithopter.*

TOP RIGHT *Concept art of a Spice Blow.*

TOOLS OF THE TRADE

Your survival will depend on your ability to adapt to your environment and to master the tools, weapons, and abilities that will aid you in your journey. "You're unlocking these different layers as you go, unlocking bigger and more complex items and abilities along the way, in a way that builds up your confidence as you progress," says Sam Rappaport. "In the beginning of the game, you're spending a lot of time walking until you can build a very basic sandbike that is only effective for getting you from one rock to another rock, then it will break down. You have to maintain it and figure out how to get better tools to make better sandbikes, then you move on to dune buggies, then ornithopters, things like that. It's a very good way of gating people.

"As a player, you always have the ability to traverse to get to a much more difficult and complicated endgame space on the map, but you're kind of gated by the type of equipment you have. That provides a more organic gaming experience, with limitations based on your current resources and abilities. Figuring out how it's going to work mechanically in the game while staying true to the lore, that was very important. If two players are on sandbikes and they know that the sandworm is going to surface and the players go off in different directions, how is that going to work as far as the gameplay is concerned? It was interesting to work through those things as we built up to higher-level items."

The most vital technology in terms of your survival is the stillsuit, one of the most iconic items in the Dune universe. Frank Herbert's original *Dune* glossary defines it as a "body-enclosing garment" of Fremen design that performs the "functions of heat dissipation and filtering bodily wastes," as well as retaining and reclaiming moisture. A properly fitted, fully functional stillsuit is literally the difference between life and death for the people of Arrakis, and your ability to master and maintain the stillsuit and its functions is essential to your quest.

"One of the things that everyone remembers about Dune, even if they have a passing knowledge, is 'isn't that the movie where people wear suits that recycle their urine and their poop?'" observes Barnaby Legg. "It's such a weird idea, but it shows you the level of thought that Frank Herbert put into the creation of his universe, that he knew people would need to recycle their fluids in these stillsuits in order to survive. That's how precious resources are on Arrakis. Not one drop of moisture should be wasted. And that, for me, feels like the perfect setup for a survival mechanic in a game. Every resource is precious. Everything is earned. Everything has its place in the ecosystem of survival."

PAGES 134-135 *Mechanics offering services along a vendor street in nighttime Harko Village.*

OPPOSITE *High-resolution character screenshots depicting a variety of in-game outfits.*

Players will need to take full advantage of Arrakeen technology to tap into those resources and to survive its inhospitable climate. The collection of the planet's two most valuable commodities, water and Spice, is paramount. "My favorite tool is probably the dew reaper, a scythe-like device that, when you sweep it across flower fields, sucks the moisture off them," says Joel Bylos, who suggested that the strange Arrakeen implement would be a welcome addition to the *Dune: Awakening* tool kit. "When you use it in the game and the water gets sucked off the tops of these fields of flowers and flows behind the blade of the reaper and gets sucked into the handle, when I play these things, I think, 'no other game in the world has this.' That, to me, is what makes our game so interesting. Those details.

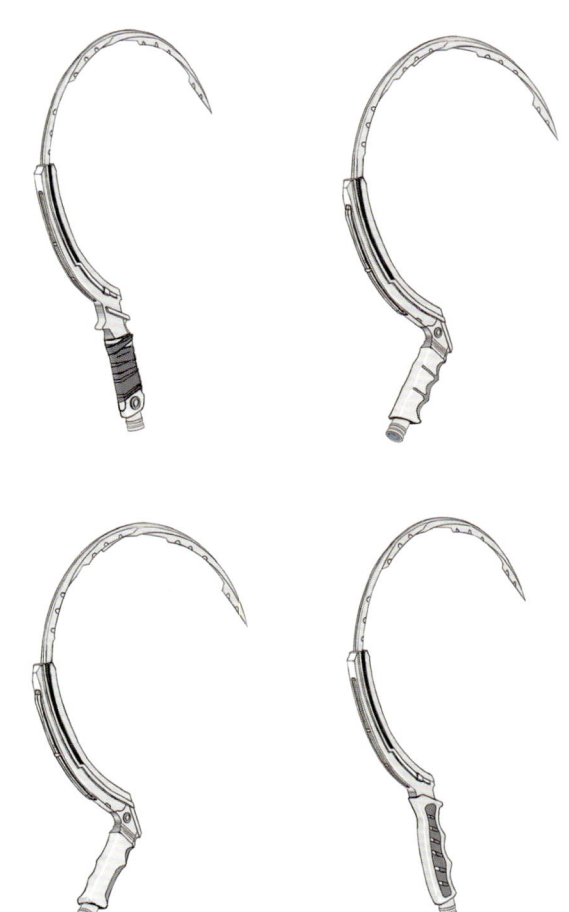

TOP LEFT *Exploratory iterations of the dew reaper.*
TOP RIGHT *Renders of a CHOAM dew reaper.*
BELOW *Renders of an Arrakeen stillsuit.*

FRONT VIEW

BACK VIEW

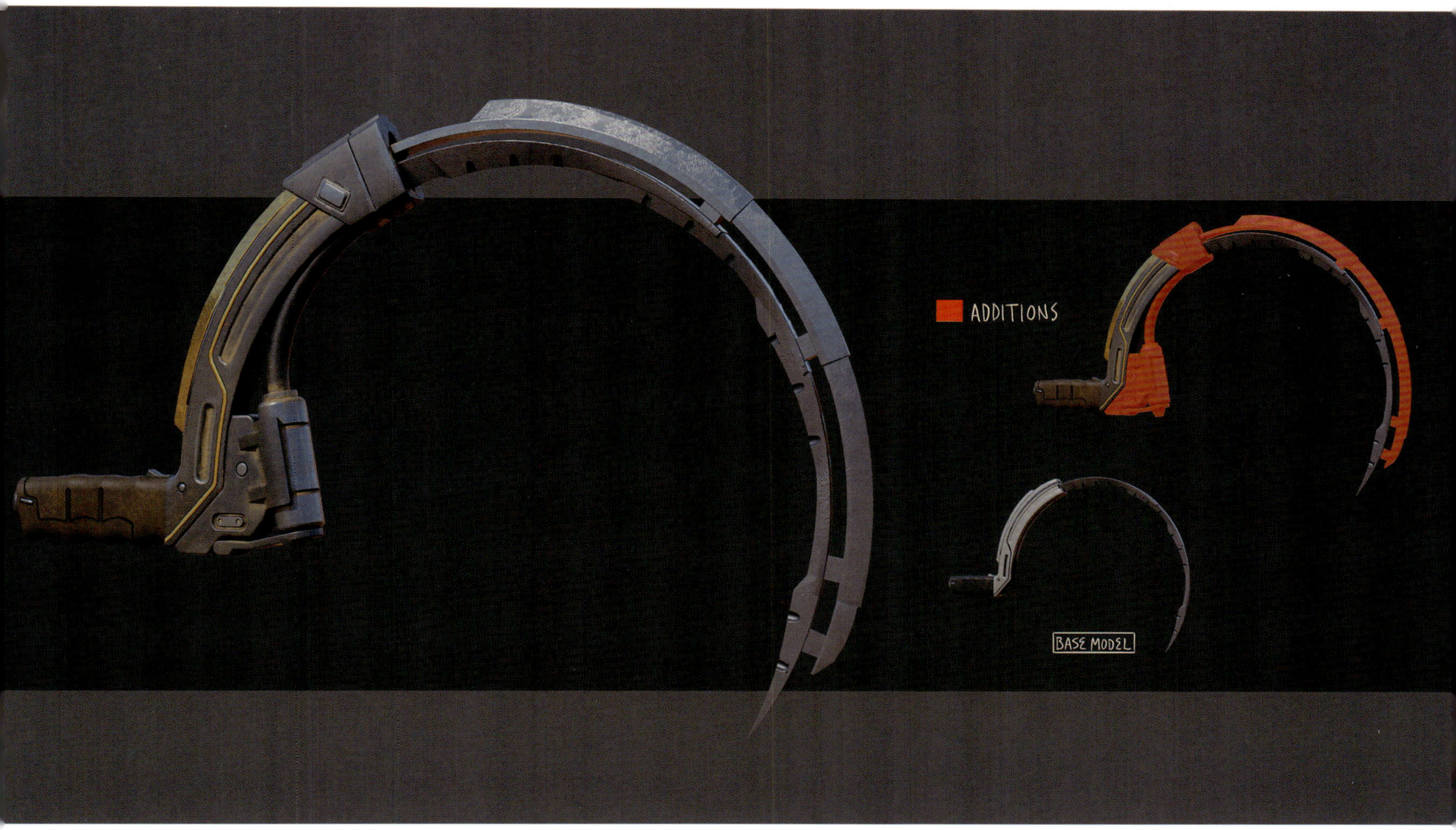

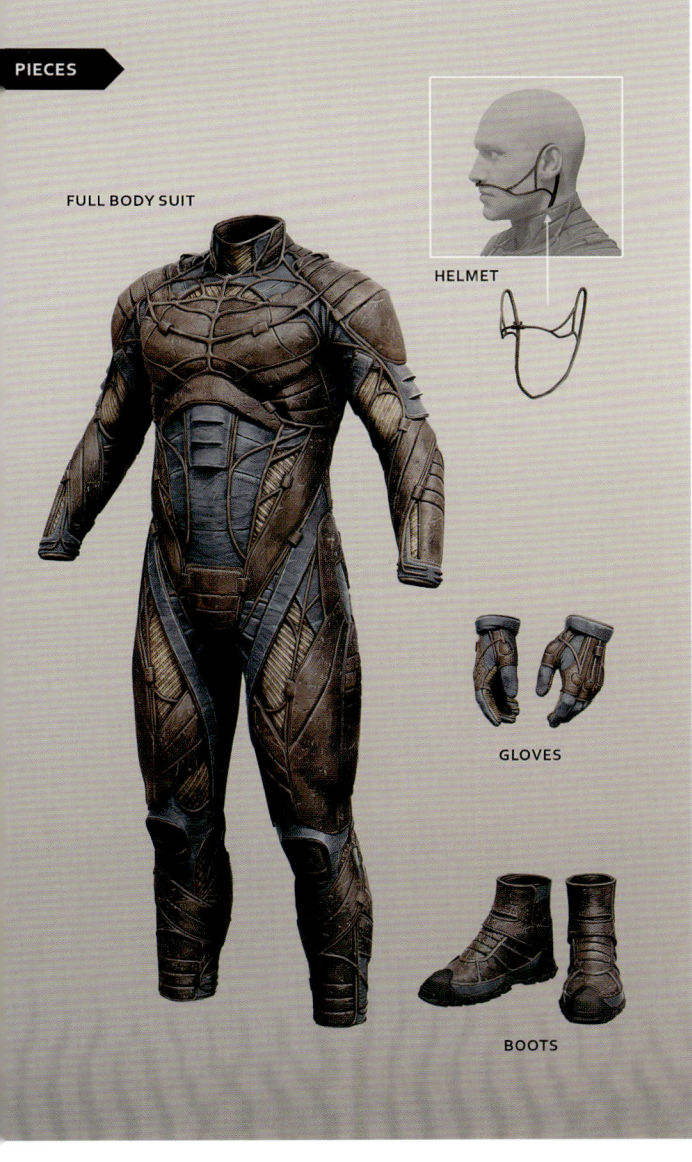

ADDITIONS

BASE MODEL

PIECES

FULL BODY SUIT

HELMET

GLOVES

BOOTS

"We also have the cutteray, the laser mining device. You do have other games with devices like that, so we tried to find our own twist on it. The static compactor, used to push the sand around. We've got one of those that's used to capture Spice and gather it into piles. Making sure these feel unique and interesting so that even if you're doing something similar to what you've seen in other games, you'll feel that you're doing something in such a way that it's unique to Dune."

Those "unique to Dune" experiences will put players to the test in ways they could have never imagined, according to Bylos. "The player undergoes a series of trials when they arrive on Arrakis, as the Spice starts to get into their bloodstream. They start to have these strange dreams, which lead them to a cave. And in that cave, they have a revelation about this Fremen item called the stillsuit. We really tried to put a lot of importance on this in the game. It's not just an item like any other item. You basically have to be tripping on Spice and go to this location to get into the spirituality of the Fremen and read these runes on the walls, these altars, where you can see an image of the stillsuit in the background. It opens your mind to the concept of the stillsuit. And then the players get access to that. And then they build it.

Tools of the Trade

CUTTERAY

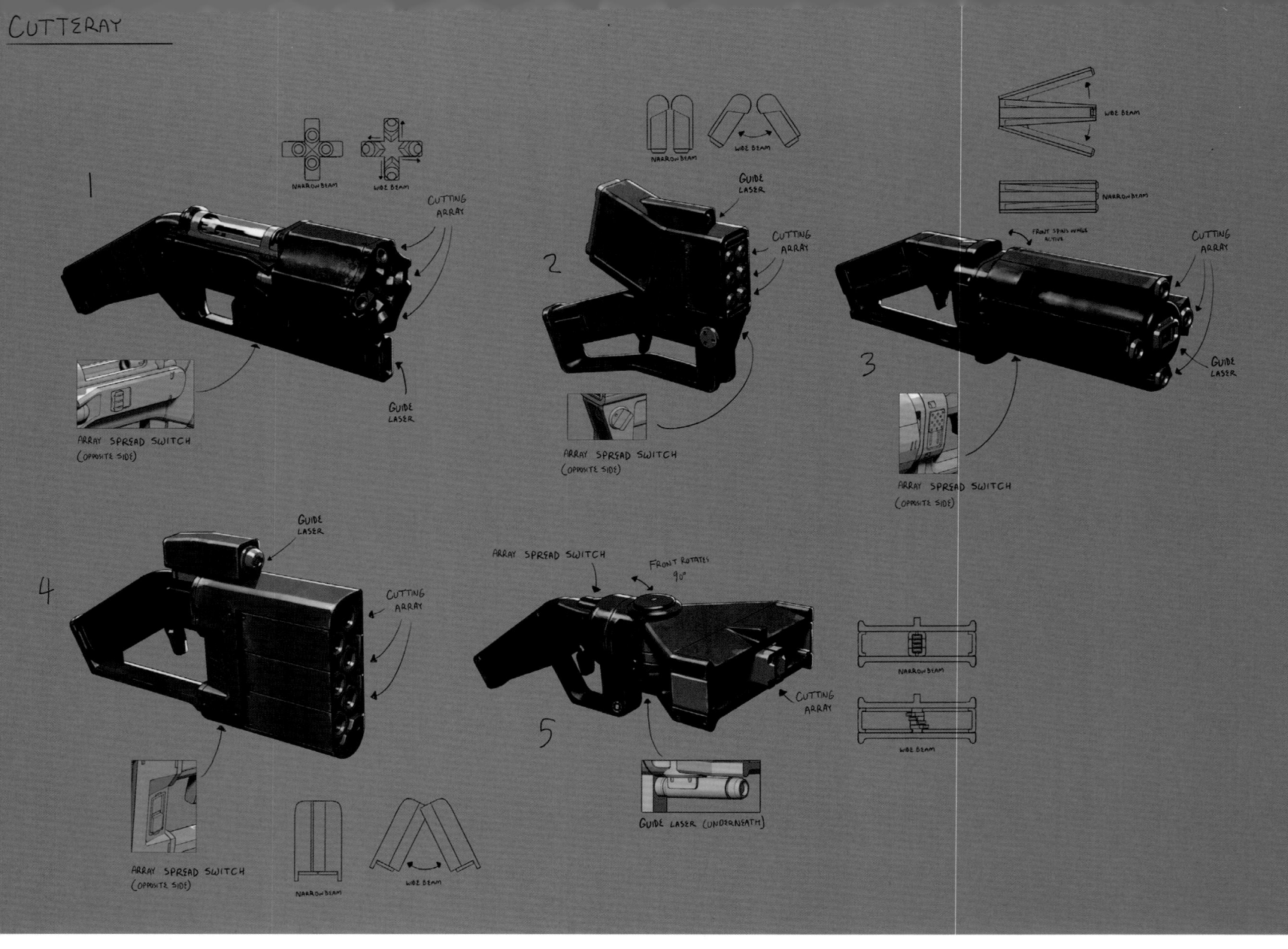

ABOVE Cutteray sketches.

OPPOSITE TOP Renders of binoculars.

OPPOSITE BOTTOM LEFT Renders of a capsule shooter.

OPPOSITE BOTTOM RIGHT Marked-up renders of a CHOAM thumper.

"The first time they put it on, there's a scene of them adjusting it and tightening it, a very important scene in the book and in the movie. Making sure the stillsuit fits correctly. And they're terrible at it, since they just started the game and they're not actually Fremen, but still, we give it all this reverence," observes Bylos. "Once you have a stillsuit, you're able to explore a lot more on Arrakis. If you have normal clothing, you're hurt by the sun and you're losing moisture.

"We have a water bar that measures your level of hydration. But when you get the stillsuit, as you lose water, you gain water. It's an interesting concept that fits with the Dune universe. As you sweat, as you perspire, urinate, whatever you're doing inside your stillsuit, it's being filtered and is filling up this other water bar that you can drink from. It's an interesting mechanic unlike anything seen in any other game. It's so iconic to Dune. And we haven't even reached the Fremen stillsuit in the game yet; that's going to be the most spectacular one.

"The other thing you have to pay attention to as a player is sunstroke and heat," Bylos continues. "In the top middle of the user interface, we've got positioned the readout, including vitals such as sunstroke. The longer you stay in the sunlight, the more chance you have of getting into this sunstroke state, which gives you a debuff. That means your water goes down much faster than it normally would. That means you'll need to drink more often. Stick to the shadows, avoid the sun. It will eventually wear off if you stay in the shade long enough."

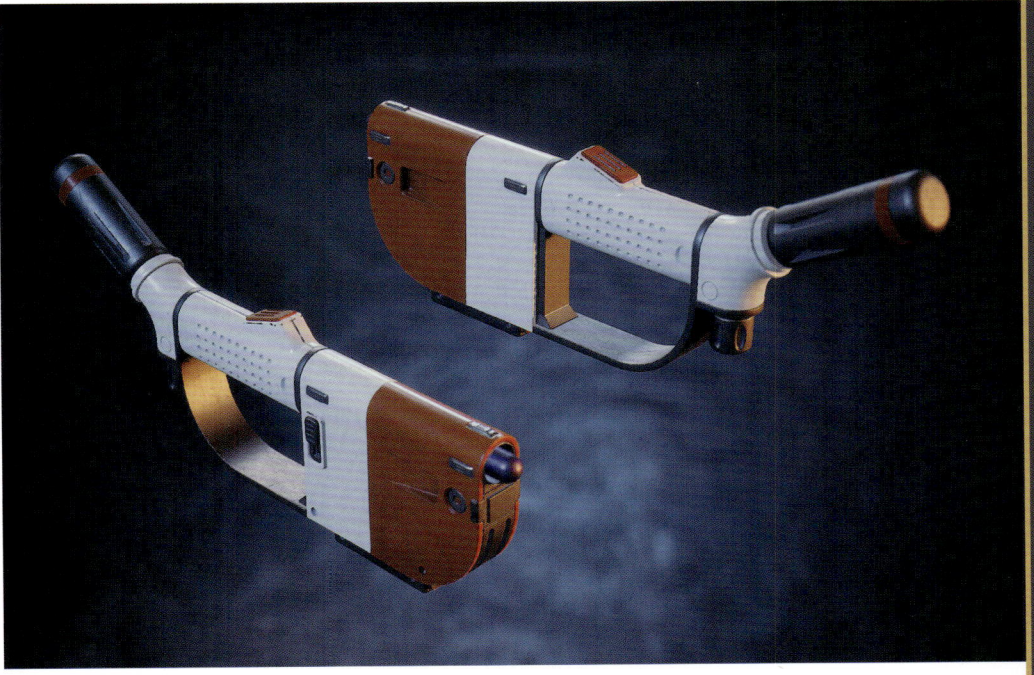

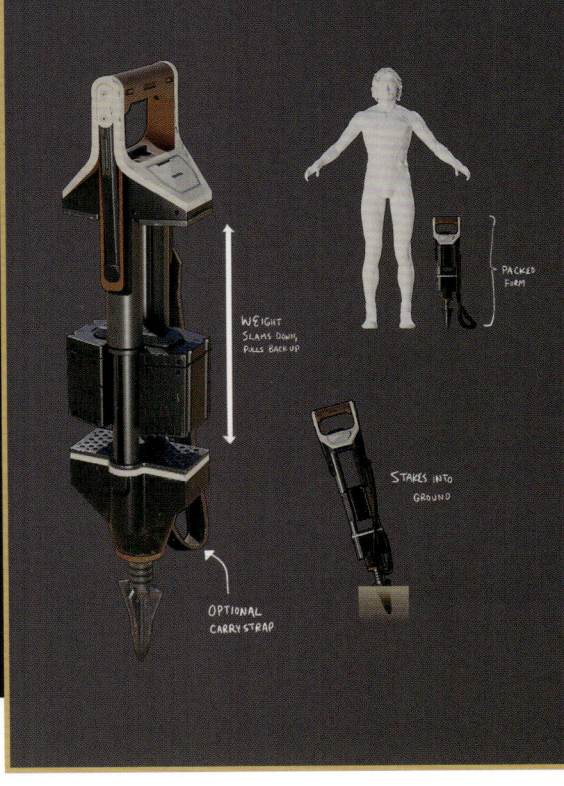

WEIGHT SLAMS DOWN, FALLS BACK UP

PACKED FORM

STAKES INTO GROUND

OPTIONAL CARRY STRAP

Those familiar with Dune lore know that the fallen, be they friend or foe, are part of the circle of life on Arrakis, where not one resource, not one drop of moisture is wasted . . . even blood. "Harvesting the blood was an idea that Funcom found in the deeper canon of the books," says Barnaby Legg. "Something that we'd seen in the movies, harvesting moisture and water from the human body, but the idea that now gamers can go one step further and become these Arrakis vampires, plunging their equipment into the veins of their fallen victims to harvest their blood and get the water from that—pretty badass."

Tools of the Trade 141

BELOW *Marked-up renders of a one-handed (top) and two-handed (bottom) Harkonnen blood extractor.*

OPPOSITE TOP *Renders of a Fremkit, a pack designed to allow Fremen to survive in the open desert.*

OPPOSITE MIDDLE, BOTTOM *Renders of several differently sized water cisterns.*

That process, known as exsanguination, can aid your survival, but it is not without risk, or cost. "Once you've defeated your enemies in battle, sometimes you've got to take their blood," notes Joel Bylos. "In order to get water, the players have to craft themselves a blood sack and a blood extractor to harvest blood from their fallen enemies. It's not always a good thing to just take blood from people—it's potentially bad and can only be used for certain things. Once you've extracted the blood, you can then of course drink it. As you'll see here, the player takes a big sip from their blood bag, but when they do, it causes a debuff because the blood is not exactly pure and drinking blood for water is not exactly a one-to-one scenario, so you'll see that our health bar got shorter while our water bar went up. Being a blood drinker is not always looked upon in a positive way."

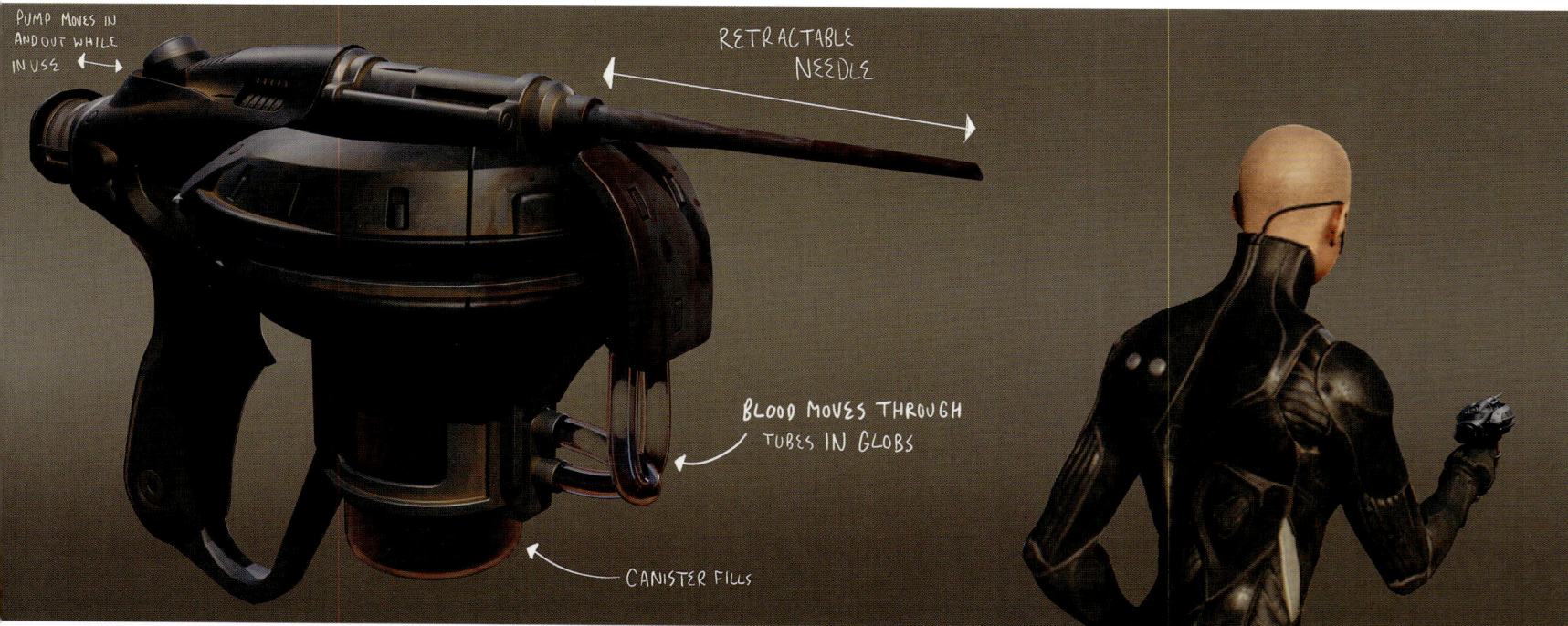

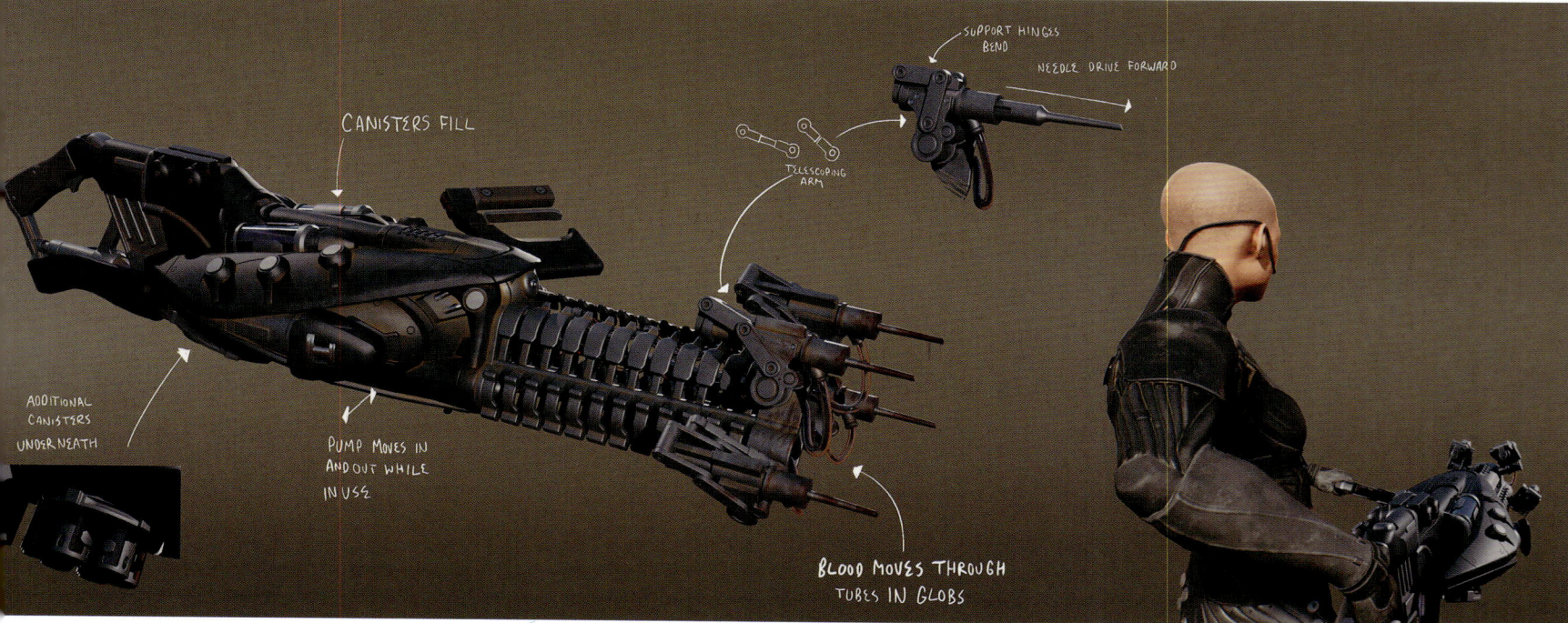

Tools of the Trade

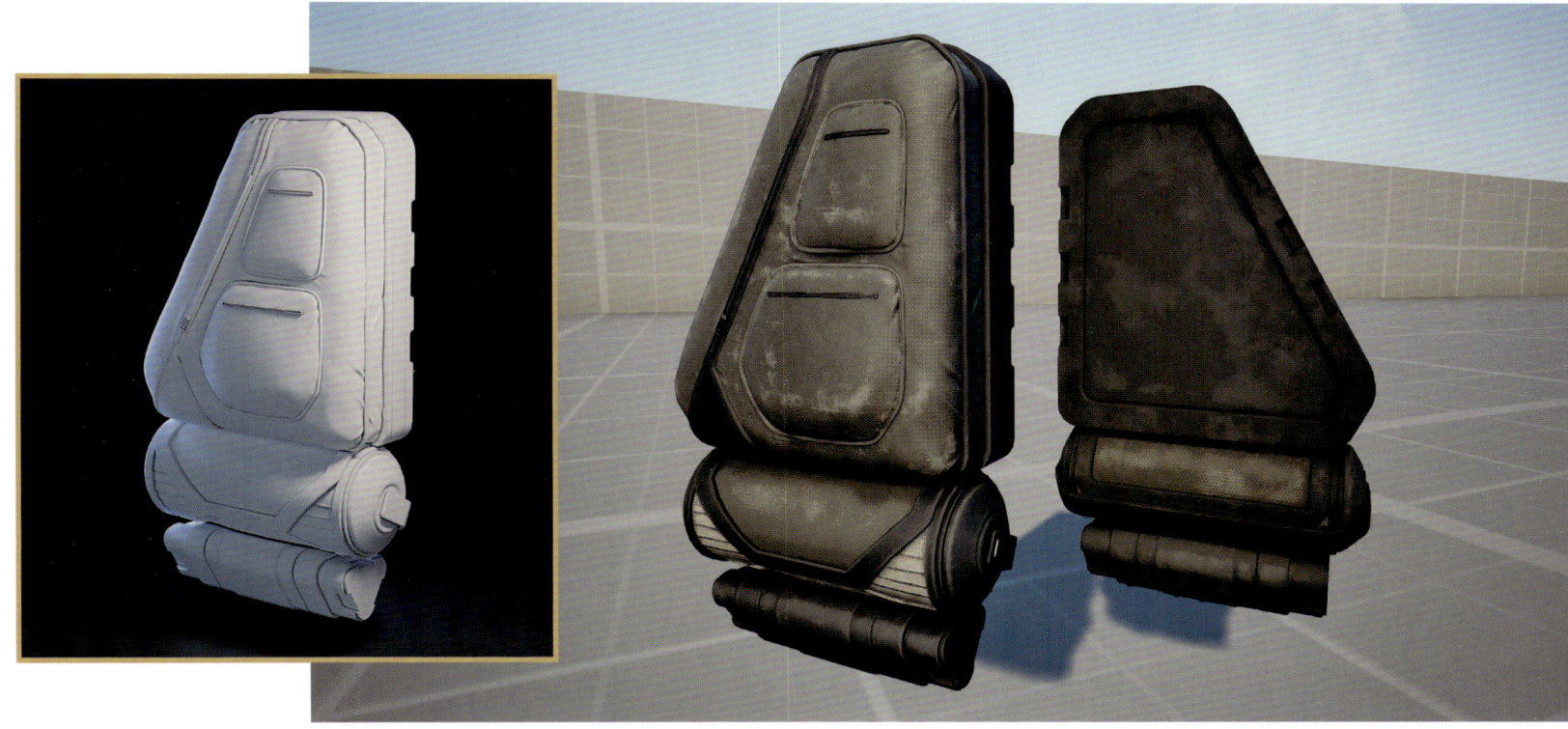

Survival includes constantly monitoring your health and vitality so that you can avoid the perils of dehydration and sunstroke, as well as the inevitable physical damage resulting from combat as you make your way through the cities and ruins of Arrakis. One of your earliest discoveries will be an abandoned cave filled with artifacts and remnants of ancient Fremen culture. "Here amongst the dead, the first question they should be asking is, what happened here? Who are these people?" says Bylos. "In this location, we give players a little bit of time to adjust their settings, get a feel for the movement keys, and then move forward into the cave, and they'll stumble upon their first major interaction point, which is the Fremkit, which serves as both a backpack for the player, of course, but also really a guide. The Fremen used to pack these with interesting objects that they could use to survive in the desert, and it's not different for the player. Here they begin their first crafting experience, crafting a small scrap out of metal that was in the Fremkit.

"The caves have been moisture-sealed to preserve the moisture of those within the cave, and so the player, as they explore, will be able to use their scrap-metal knife to pierce the seals and escape. So really this entire area built using Unreal Engine 5 is just to sort of [ease the player] into the path. A lot of survival games have very abrupt, very harsh beginnings, and we tried to make the experience of joining Dune: Awakening just a little easier. Just give people a little bit of a feel for the world before we really toss them out into the harshness that is the desert of Arrakis."

TOP GEAR

Your skill level, abilities, and access to technology will grow as you progress. As your stamina increases, so does your ability to reach areas that would have been inaccessible without your free-form climbing system and suspensor belts, which the official *Dune* glossary describes as "hovering" devices that utilize the "secondary (low-drain) phase of a Holtzman field generator" to nullify gravity "within certain limits prescribed by relative mass and energy consumption."

Each new item and ability further unlocks gameplay potential, from the survival gear, including the Fremkit, stillsuit, and the stilltent, which can provide shelter quickly and efficiently; defensive items like the Holtzman shield; implements valuable for traversal such as the Shigawire Claw; and weaponry including daggers, swords, and handheld devices that fire projectiles. "From an equipment perspective, we never wanted this to be a *Call of Duty*–style run-and-gun shooter, but obviously we wanted to have both melee content and other advanced weaponry in the game, so making those things feel very mechanical in the way that Dune is, because there's no gunpowder in that world," Sam Rappaport observes. "There are gas-powered and spring-powered guns, so you have to use creative design and sound design to make weapons that work within the lore. Looking at concepts that are heavy with springs or gas-powered canisters, that guided the team in that direction.

"We had to make a few changes to established lore, though," he continues. "If you fire a lasgun at someone who has their shield activated in the books, it makes this massive nuclear explosion. Which is a very cool idea, but we can't have that in the game, with players destroying the entire map every time that happens. Coming up with clever narrative solutions to those types of things was very fun."

ABOVE *Concept art of a CHOAM stilltent.*

OPPOSITE TOP *Suspensor belts reduce or nullify the influence of gravity on the user.*

OPPOSITE BOTTOM *Sketches of CHOAM suspensor belts.*

SUSPENSOR CLIP

ACTIVATION DIAL

COILS GLOW BRIGHTER WHILE IN USE

ON BUTTON

VENTS GLOW BRIGHTER WHILE IN USE

SAFETY BUTTON

TURN TO ACTIVATE

VENTS GLOW WHILE IN USE

SETTINGS

PANELS SHIMMER WHILE IN USE

ACTIVATOR SWITCH

LIGHTS GLOW ON USE, STEAM EMITS

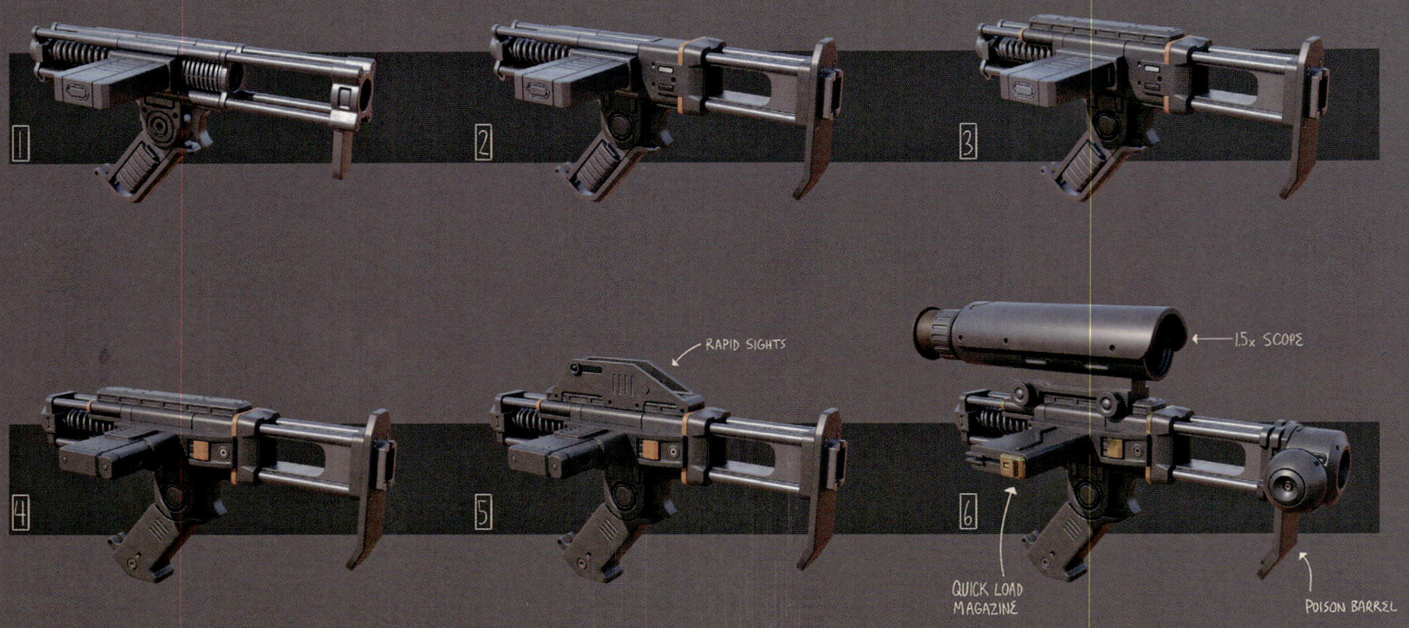

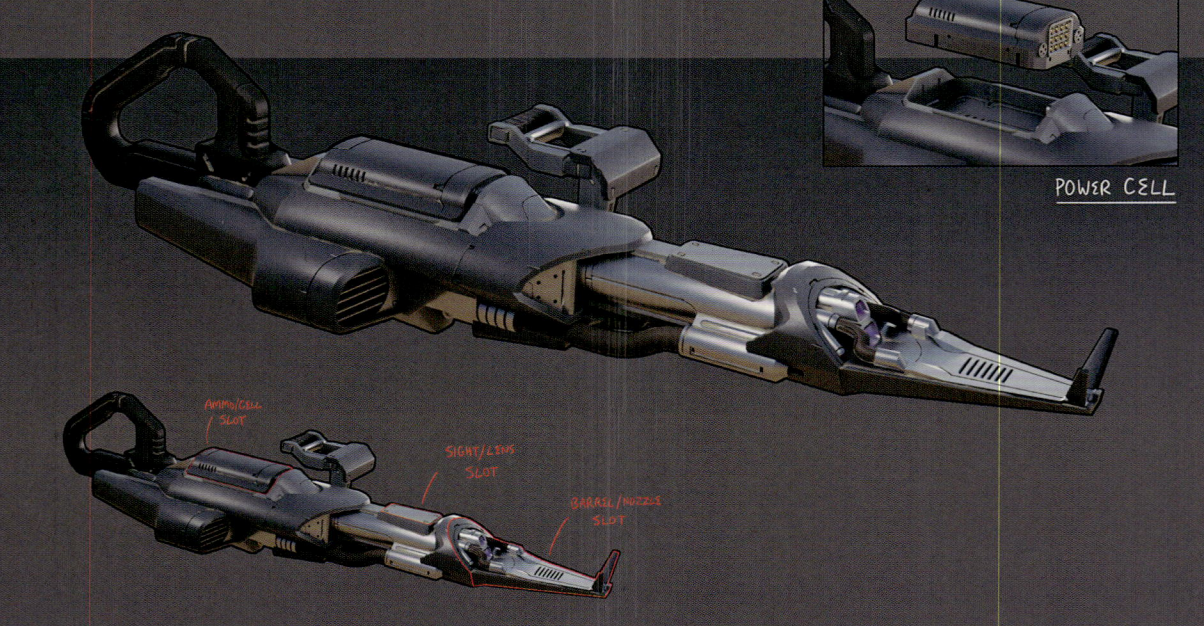

CHOAM HEAVY LASGUN

POWER CELL

ATREIDES DAGGER

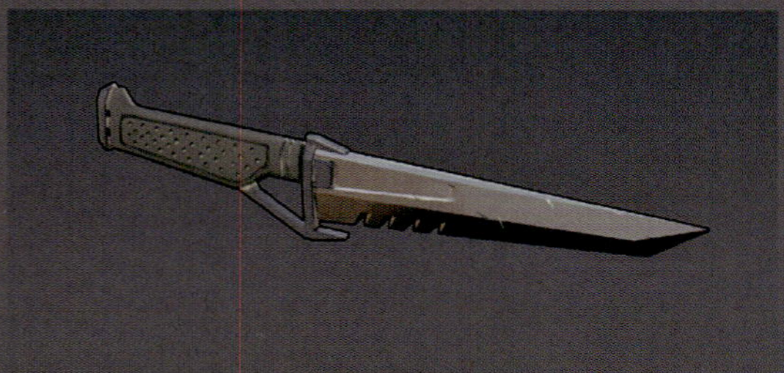

CHOAM DAGGER

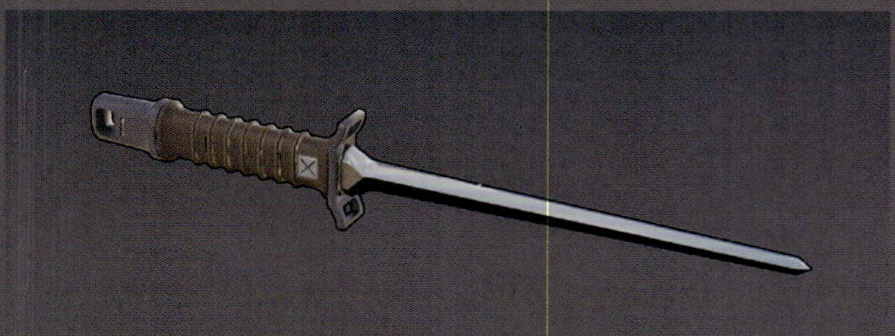

HARKONNEN DAGGERS

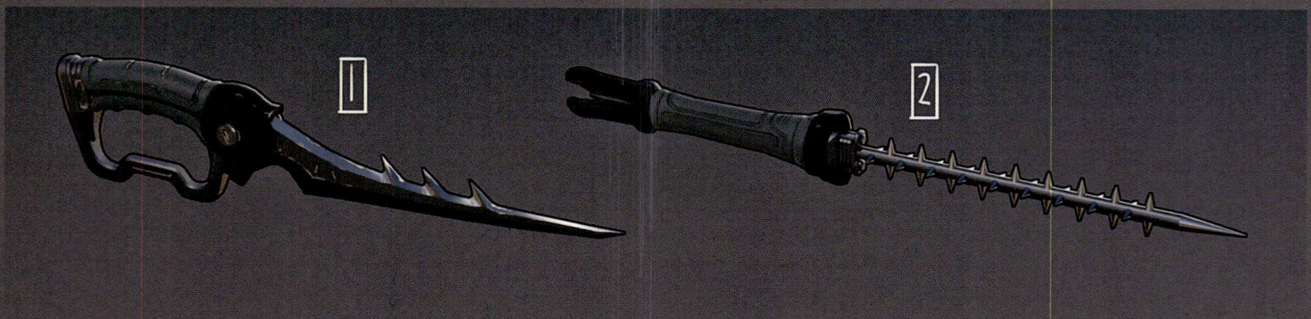

Nailing down the design and gameplay for the iconic lasgun was one of the more complicated tasks faced by David Levy and his team, who worked to find the perfect balance between form, design, functionality, and fidelity to both the original source material and Denis Villeneuve's films. "For the lasgun, we went through five or six iterations before we landed on our final design," says Levy. "Going back and forth between the books and the movies and the game, and back to the drawing board so many times.

"If you look at the weapons in the movie, a lot of them have that 'low-tech' approach to them. In the book, there are no bullets. Everything uses compressed air and mechanical devices to push projectiles through the air. The weapons are aged, mechanical, grounded in a way that feels very real, but [they] also have a futuristic vibe to them.

"The great thing about the game is that you can create a truly fantastic array of weapons that will not even be used by the players," he continues. "You can really have fun with that, where you take a sword or a rapier, close-combat weapons, or a magnetic mine, which is much more adapted to the conventional game environment. Being able to have that range was so much fun. Rusted, aged, damaged, used for hundreds of years . . . it was very enjoyable to design those."

Although several of the items and weapons in *Dune: Awakening* are unique to the game, many were brought to life by the talented armorers and craftspeople who developed the visual language of Denis Villeneuve's *Dune* films, and great care was taken when adapting those from one medium to another. The game developers took note of the care and detail found in each and every item crafted for the films and strove to bring that same attention to detail to *Dune: Awakening*. "The team put so much effort into every detail of the game," observes Sam Rappaport. "Every crysknife is unique to a different person. When you get to hold those on set and see them in person, you see that each one is etched differently and is unique to its owner. That is very cool, and that is something that we're trying to bring into the game as well.

"Technology evolved differently on Arrakis, and that's reflected in the other weapons and items as well," he continues. "The suspensor technology is very cool. The shield belt and the activator that you wear on your wrist, we got to play with all of that stuff on set. One of the big things that we tried to bring into the game based on what we saw on the set is that you see all of these different types of weaponry that different factions have. You have all of these visual cues that separate one faction from another, so it's cool to see all the swords and daggers, the shortblades and the longblades, the Maula pistols.

"It's very cool to have seen that stuff on set and then to bring it into the game and make it as 'Duney' as possible. The shield technology in the game is so cool because it's exactly like you experience in the films, with the bluish-whitish glow when something's not penetrating, but once the slow blade penetrates the shield, it starts to turn red in that area."

OPPOSITE *Sketches of a variety of firearms and melee weapons available in the game. From top to bottom: CHOAM Maula pistol tier progression, a CHOAM heavy lasgun, Atreides and CHOAM daggers, and Harkonnen daggers.*

A full complement of weapons and equipment will be necessary for each player to navigate the terrain and to access every corner of each player hub they visit. "The cutteray is what we use to analyze structures to find their weak points," Joel Bylos notes, describing one of the handheld tools that are essential to survival and exploration. "Then we cut along those lines to break open the structures and gain the resources inside. This is like mining, and we apply it both to the rocks and to the metals in the game. At the start of the game, you'll be scanning around and picking up . . . rocks that you can harvest. Breaking them apart and taking those pieces with you.

"With the world broken apart by the War of Assassins, the NPC bases are scattered all over Arrakis. We're switching to a character who's slightly more advanced, and he's using his binoculars to mark an NPC outpost. That marker will then appear on our compass, and you're able to approach them in any way you like. In this case, you will want to use a Shigawire Claw combined with a suspensor belt to get up to high ground and approach the enemy base from above. One of the interesting things about *Dune: Awakening* is how you can combine the different abilities, and this is how traversal really plays into the game. You can attack these bases from any angle that you'd like now."

For offensive capabilities, you will craft the first gun in the game, known as a Maula pistol, or M pistol, defined by Frank

TOP LEFT *Atreides SMG tier progression.*

TOP RIGHT *Sketches of a CHOAM flamethrower.*

BOTTOM *Smuggler scattergun tier progression.*

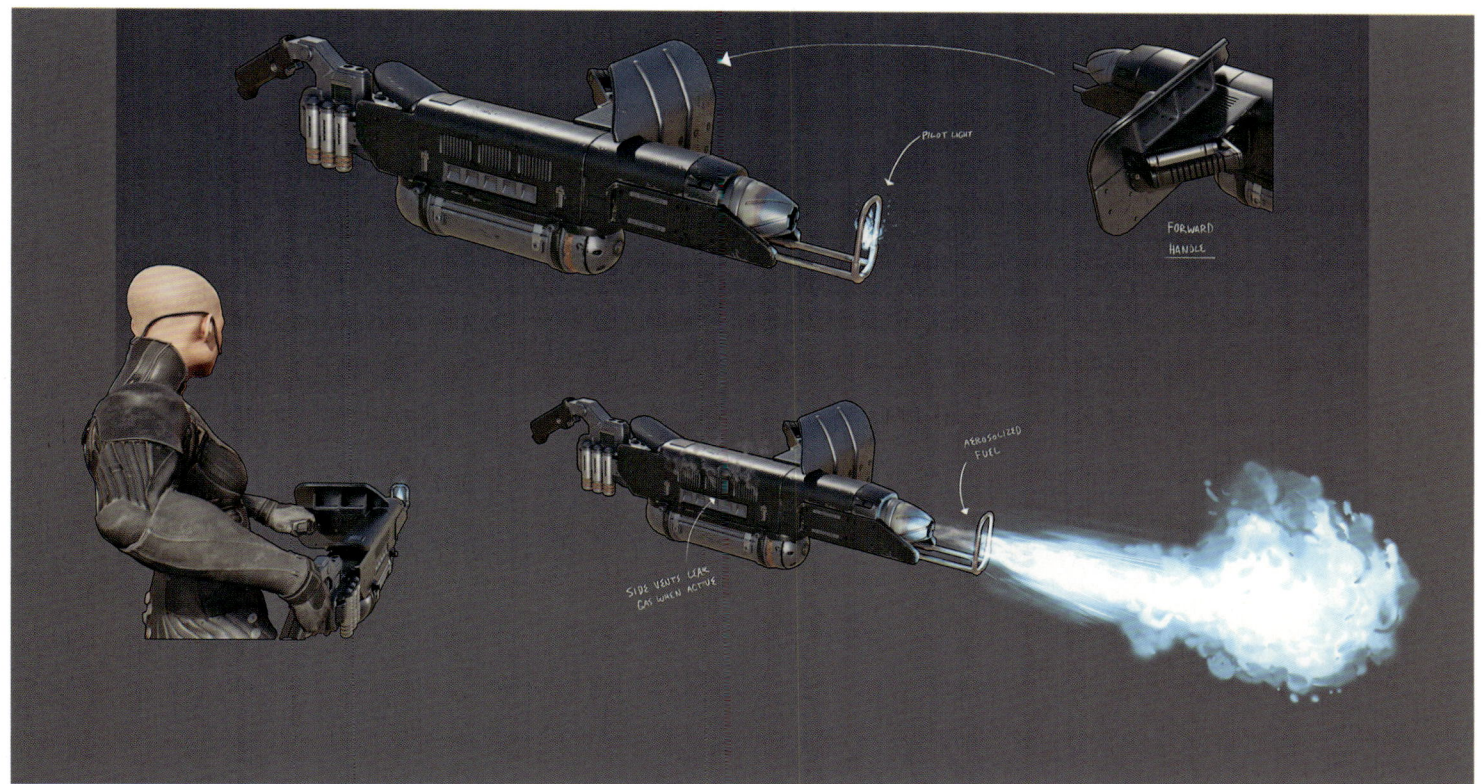

Herbert as a "spring-loaded gun for firing poison darts; range about 40 metres." Gunpowder does not exist on Arrakis, Bylos notes, and the weapons found on the planet have evolved accordingly. "Bullets are not the preferred type of ammunition. Instead, t's darts, which are fired at a slower rate in order to try and attempt to pierce shields. Enemies don't really have shields early in the game, but you can use a combination of their early abilities with tools, including the Shigawire Claws and suspensor belts, to develop an effective style of combat against the NPCs known as Troopers, the basic shock troops of the universe. *Dune: Awakening* is at heart a third-person shooter with melee and abilities, and it's the combination of melee abilities and ranged shooting that creates what we call combined arms in the game."

Designing the shields for the NPCs as well as the playable characters in *Dune: Awakening* presented a unique challenge to Funcom as they attempted to strike a balance between effects that were practical in the film adaptations and those that would enhance and facilitate gameplay. "Of course, the tone and the mood and the atmosphere in the movies are a big inspiration to us," says Morgan Sandbæk. "It's something we tried to replicate on the lighting side for a long time to sort of try to utilize some of that monochromatic look, their moods. We studied the new film when looking at the Holtzman shields, since each took such a different approach to that technology.

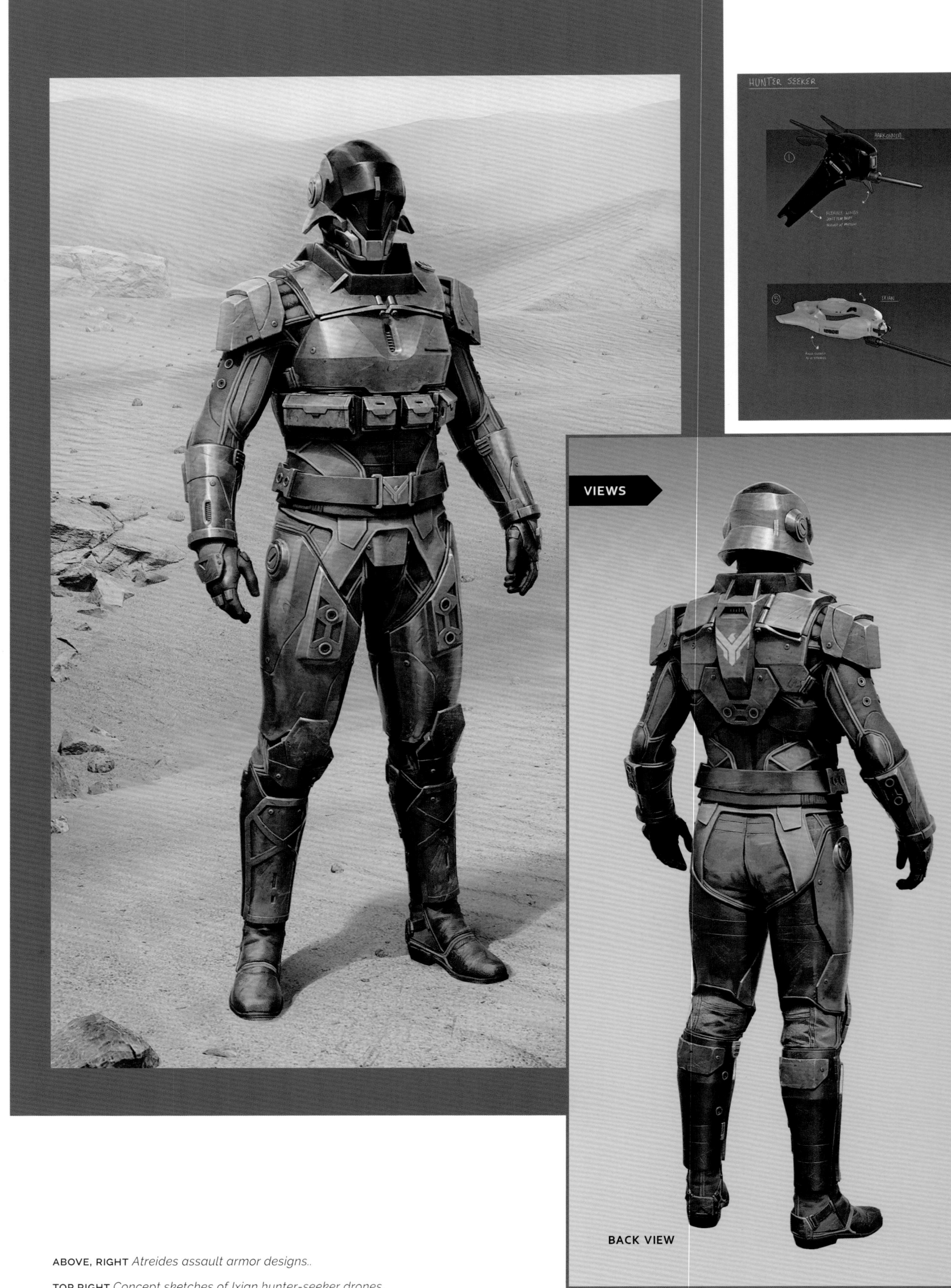

ABOVE, RIGHT *Atreides assault armor designs..*

TOP RIGHT *Concept sketches of Ixian hunter-seeker drones.*

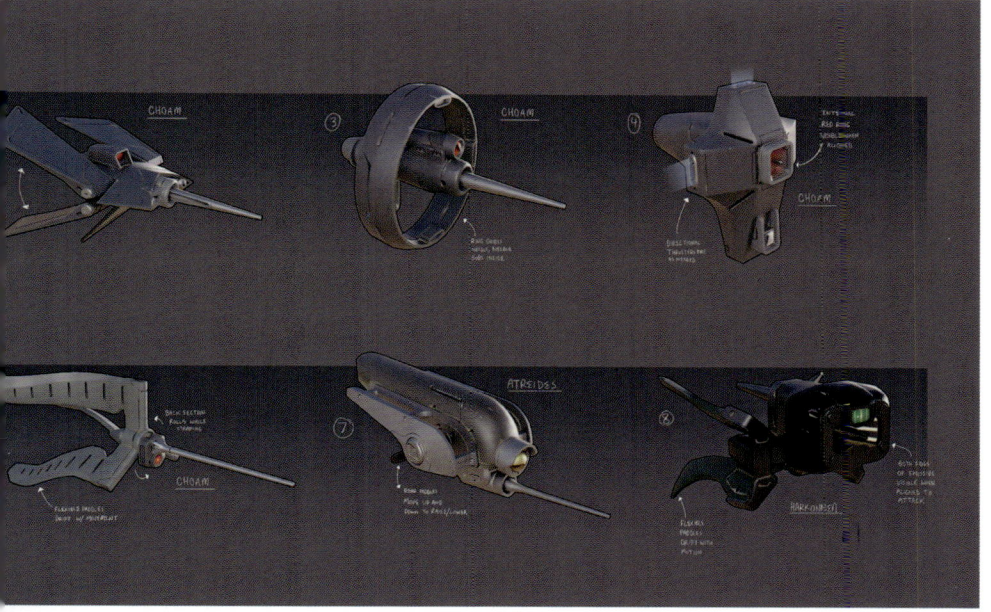

SIDE VIEW

"Also, we're more heavily influenced by the latest films because it's also what players or people would expect from a modern Dune production. It's like they really set the standard and we're trying to match it or sort of work with it to put it that way. And do our own thing, but not like something completely different."

Battle damage is inevitable whether you are shielded or not. Health kits and bandages will be as fundamental to your ongoing survival as your cache of weapons. "When you've taken a fair amount of damage in this battle, it's important to stop and heal using a bandage," says Joel Bylos. "Bandages heal over time, so you can't just heal yourself up to 100 percent instantly. You have to actually get into safety. Get behind cover before you start using them, or you may find yourself in a perilous situation such as fighting against a Swordmaster.

"When enemies have shields, melee is a much more emphasized style of combat. You hear that and you see that when a player is not really equipped to handle ranged characters; they have to fall back on their abilities to get in close. Your advanced abilities, however, include Battlefield Calculation. If you tap into your Mentat training, you will be able to calculate from anybody to see what they're carrying and what they're wearing. Armed with that knowledge, you will know when to utilize talents like the hunter-seeker ability to take down enemies in the world really quickly." A hunter-seeker, in Dune lore, is a ravening sliver of suspensor-buoyed metal guided as a weapon by a nearby control console: a common assassination device. Floating in midair, it kills by entering the body and following nerve pathways to vital organs. "Obviously, when you're playing with a friend, you want to combine your abilities and work together. You can determine if an enemy is down or not or if you want to execute them or not."

Adaptation and ingenuity are the keys to survival. Your choice of weapons and abilities determines your strategy. The iconic weapons and equipment of Arrakis are at your disposal, but to truly thrive in this inhospitable world, innovation is your greatest asset. "I think the crafting is an aspect of the game that players are going to find really satisfying," says Barnaby Legg. "There's something almost meditative about heading out into the wilderness to split a rock apart and harvest the minerals that are inside it, or to brave the Spice fields to try to bring some of that precious Melange back to your base. There's something that I think people in recent years have really come to love about crafting and survival games that is very much unusual in the massively multiplayer kind of RPG space. The idea that nothing is easily come by in Arrakis adds to that feeling that this is a world that's really going to test players. It's really true to the world of Dune."

TRAVERSAL

ATREIDES
SAND BIKE
DUNE: AWAKENING

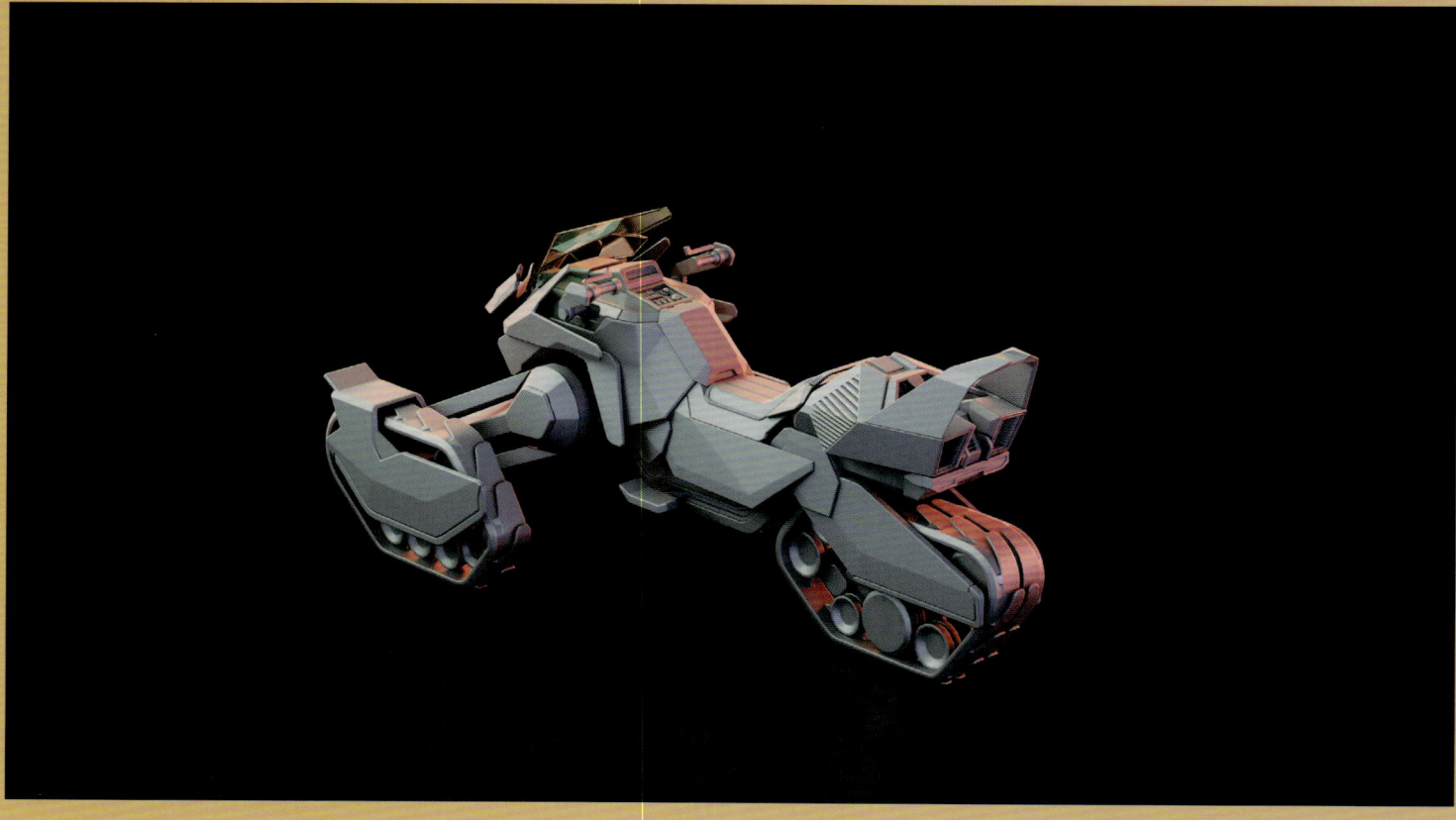

The Arrakis desert appears infinite, stretching out for miles, as far as the eye can see. The endless horizon suggests unlimited opportunity, but when you first explore the planet's surface, your range is bound by your very finite abilities. Sunstroke weakens you every moment you find yourself venturing from the safety and shade provided by the rock islands that dot the windswept landscape. Until you learn the native methods of walking without rhythm, every step you take puts you and your traveling companions at risk of awakening a sandworm and chancing a fatal encounter with the hungry leviathans. The promise of exploration seems to be forever, tantalizingly out of reach.

But just as the people of Arrakis developed and perfected use of the technology that would allow them to survive, they realized that customized vehicles specially crafted to traverse the desert plains would open up the entire world for exploration as they could evade sunstroke, sandworms, enemy factions, and other threats to their existence.

Through exploration and trade, you will acquire your first fabricator, a machine that will allow you to realize your potential and will open up the desert for exploration in ways that a lone explorer could only imagine. "One of the most exciting things is crafting yourself a vehicle," says Joel Bylos. "You can purchase the design for the first, most basic vehicle, the sandbike, early in the game.

"Each of the components is fabricated individually on a sort of 3D printer, which creates the elements that will come together to form the different pieces of the sandbike. Then we remove them from the fabricator, place them in our inventory, and use the welding tool to place out vehicle pieces. It's a cooperative activity, so any player can help with this. That's very important when it comes to crafting transport ships or sand crawlers. You can add an extra seat in case you'd like to take a passenger on the sandbike. Once it's been assembled and fueled up, you can jump on and head out into the greater world of Arrakis."

PAGES 152-153 *Concept illustration of a landed Atreides medium ornithopter.*

OPPOSITE TOP *Concept illustrations of the Atreides sandbike design.*

OPPOSITE MIDDLE, BOTTOM *Unpainted renders of front and rear views of the Atreides sandbike.*

TOP *The Atreides sandbike on the sands of Arrakis.*

BOTTOM *Unpainted rear-view render of the Harkonnen sandbike design.*

Traversal

Funcom's Associate Art Director, Karl Mario Garibay Froede, and his team oversaw the development of every vehicle in Dune: Awakening to create machines that would build upon the cinematic world established by Production Designer Patrice Vermette. "The vehicles in the movie have such an ominous presence to them, and we had to bring that same feeling to the game. The first thing that we developed was the ornithopter, since that is such an important part of the Dune world," says Froede. "In the beginning, it seemed that the vehicles would just have a side presence in the game, but they gained prominence as we progressed. It became clear very quickly that this would be a really important, really fun part of the game. People love riding on the sandbikes and flying through the sky in an ornithopter.

"Our job is making sure the vehicles meet a certain standard, that they are visually consistent with the world of the movies, but that we've got something fun, too. Believable, as grounded as possible, and that they fit into the lore of Dune. How they look and feel in the world.

"The Dune lore was created in the 1960s and 1970s by Frank Herbert, who had wild fantasies about what the future might be, and that vision has morphed and adapted over time. In the original novels, there are all sorts of vehicles, many so elaborate that they never made it into the movies. We looked to Villeneuve's movies for our visual cues, his real, brutalist structures, almost monolithic, to ask ourselves what we could bring to the player's first vehicle experience without immediately unleashing the ornithopter and opening up the gameplay that way. We felt there should be some evolution while you play so that you have a feeling of accomplishment as you progress through the game and immerse yourself in the Dune experience."

That immersion starts at the ground level, which was a very deliberate choice by the game developers. "The reasoning behind starting with the bike is giving you a cheaper, entry-level experience to help you navigate the sand but still give you something that will be fun to play," says Froede. "It's simple, but it's so much fun for the player to ride the sandbike through Arrakis. There's a lot of sand to navigate, and you have to move quickly from island to island to save yourself; otherwise, the sandworm will surface and eat you. And that was perfectly suited for the sandbike, a small, cost-effective vehicle that is easy to build and learn. And it opens up the game considerably from walking around Arrakis on foot.

OPPOSITE *The Harkonnen sandbike on the sands of Arrakis.*

RIGHT *Unpainted front-view render of the Harkonnen sandbike design.*

Traversal

TOP *The CHOAM sandbike on the sands of Arrakis.*

BOTTOM *Renders of various views of the CHOAM sandbike design.*

Empty module slot

Traversal

"I've always been a motorcycle enthusiast. The classic Ducati motorcycles, those were a great source of inspiration for me as we developed the sandbikes. I'm not an engineer, where I know the mechanics and the specifications behind the operations of the vehicles; I'm more about the overall believability of a vehicle. My job is to develop believable industrial design whether it would actually function or not. Production design, vehicle design, that's always been my main passion. Vehicles that look believable, are fun to drive, and look cool."

To live on Arrakis, you must meet every challenge that comes your way, and you must adapt in order to survive. Every day represents a new opportunity for you to level up both in terms of your own abilities and in the equipment that will aid you in your mission. "You have tiers of progression. When you upgrade from the bike, you move on to the buggy, which can transport four players, and it goes up from there," says Froede.

TOP, MIDDLE, BOTTOM *CHOAM tank.*
OPPOSITE *CHOAM buggy.*

ATREIDES
DUNE BUGGY
DUNE: AWAKENING

INVENTORY

SHIELD GENERATOR

EMPTY

BOOST

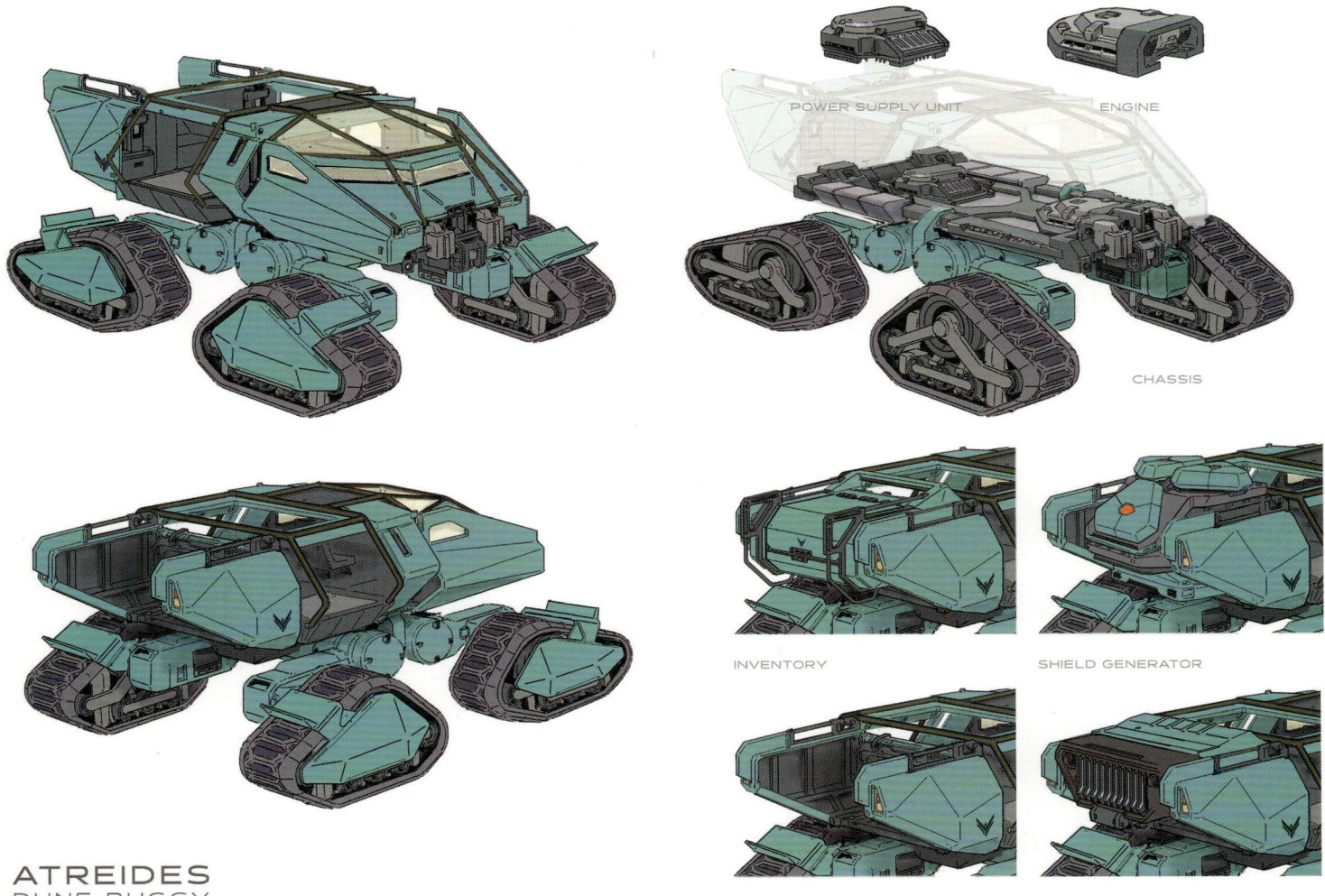

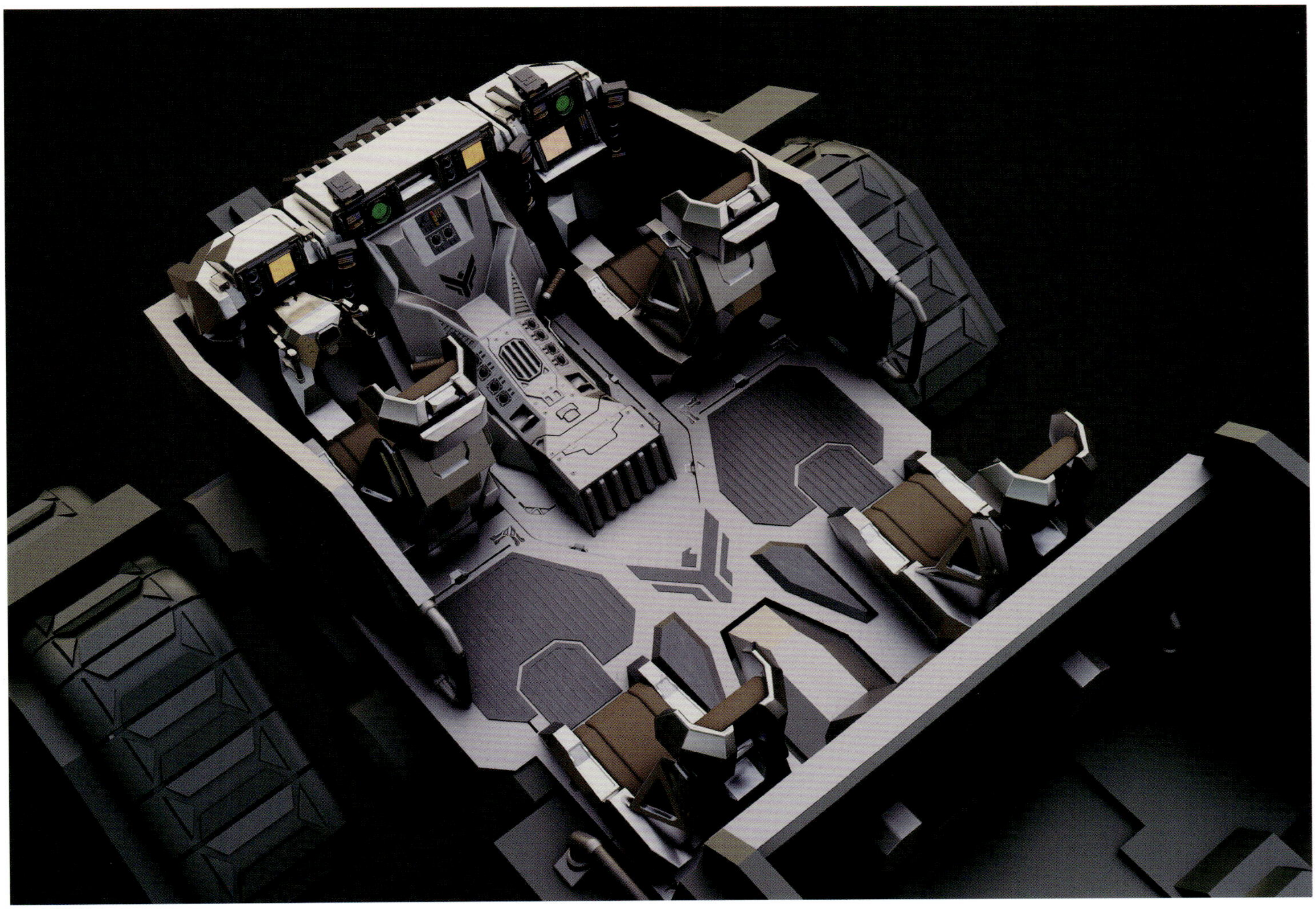

"Creating something that is somehow unique, that's the real fun for us. There are of course games like *Grand Theft Auto*, but that's to be expected. Giving the players a choice on how to move through the desert: What do we do? How much can we deviate from what people would expect from a bike or a dune buggy? I'm very confident that on each vehicle we have something very special that nobody has ever seen before. Some of them look recognizable, but in their animation and locomotion, there is something very unique, and very cool.

"Almost everything that was ever done, we looked at any kind of design. You look at real life to see what that offers, you look to the movie to see if elements have already been designed, and then you come up with your own ideas. How many games have done dune buggies? *Halo* has the most prominent dune buggy ever, so don't get too close to that one. We studied that, and *Call of Duty*, other games, to come up with something cool that's new and not derivative. We watched a lot of car races, too, motocross racing. In terms of building certain mechanics like joints and springs, we had to see what the real world offers and found ways to simulate those mechanics in a believable way but simplified for design and gameplay."

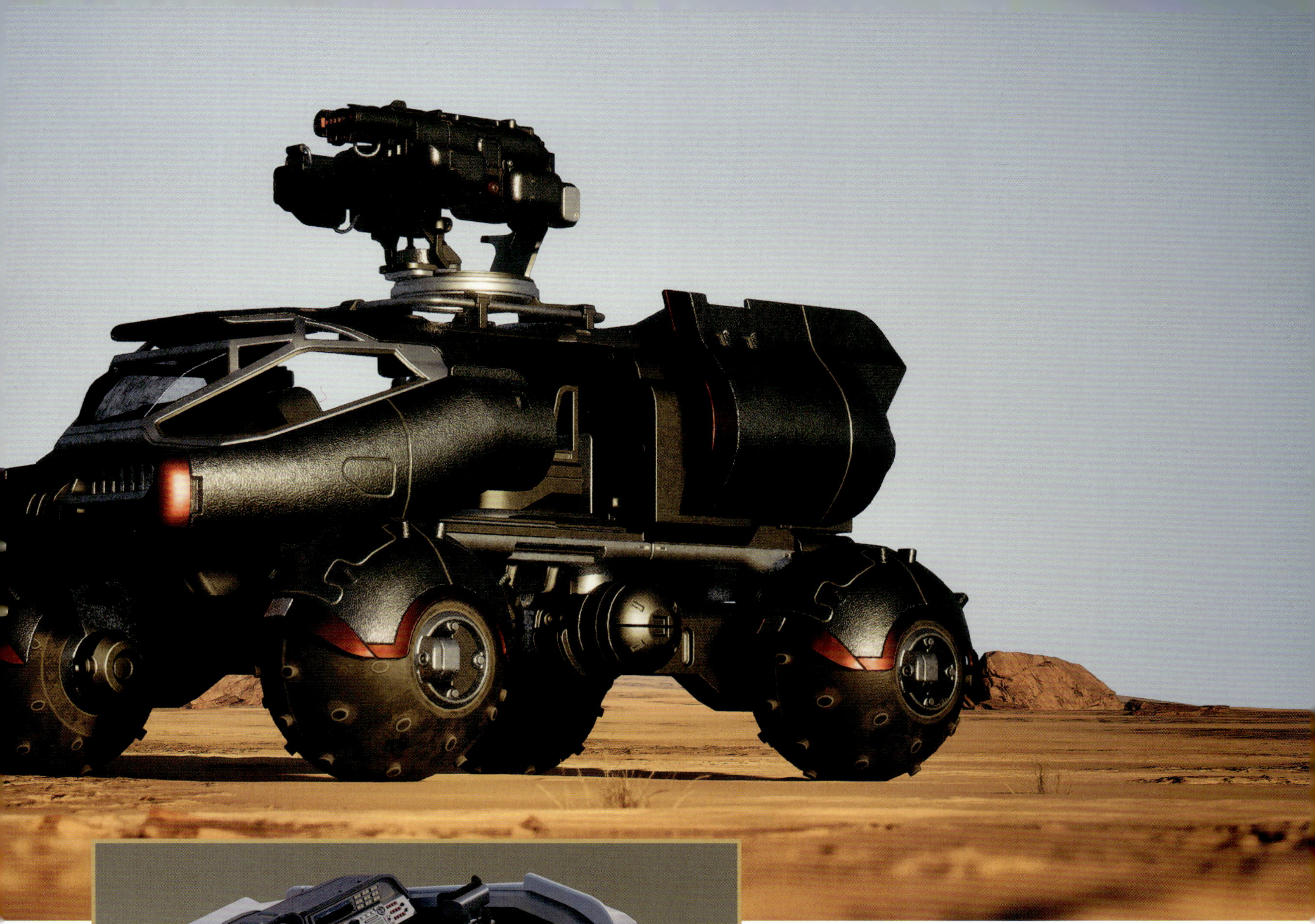

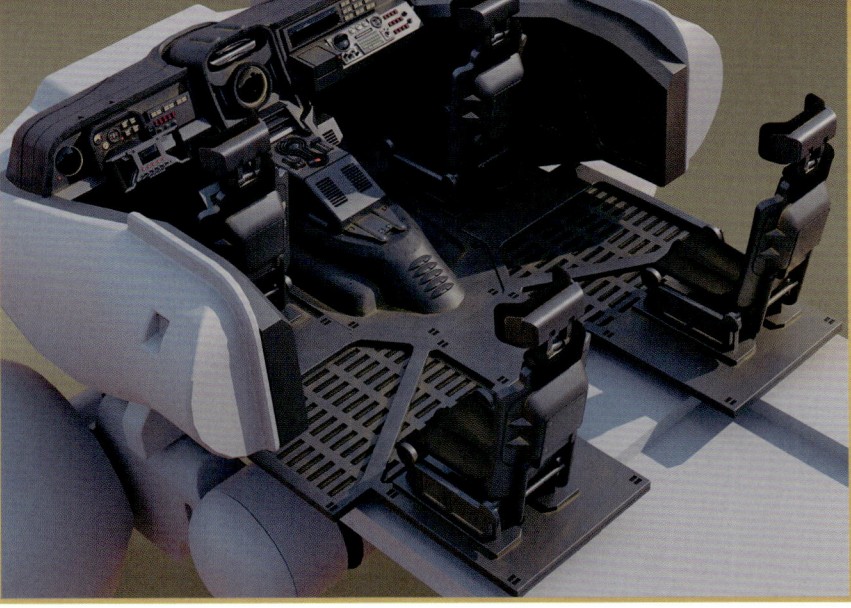

TOP, LEFT *The Harkonnen buggy on the sands of Arrakis.*

OPPOSITE *Unpainted front-view render of the Harkonnen buggy design.*

MIDDLE LEFT *Harkonnen four-seat buggy interior design.*

ABOVE *Concept illustrations of the Harkonnen buggy design.*

Traversal · 165

ABOVE *Unpainted renders of various views of the CHOAM tank.*

RIGHT *Concept illustration of the underside of the CHOAM tank.*

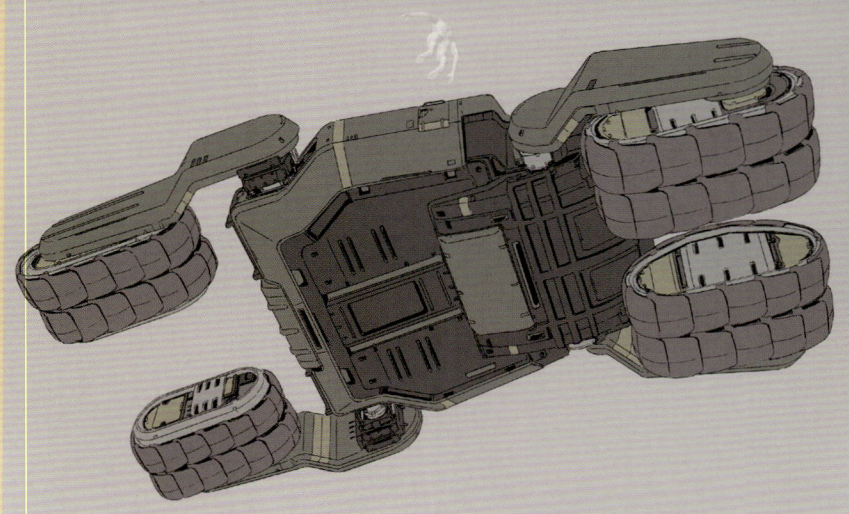

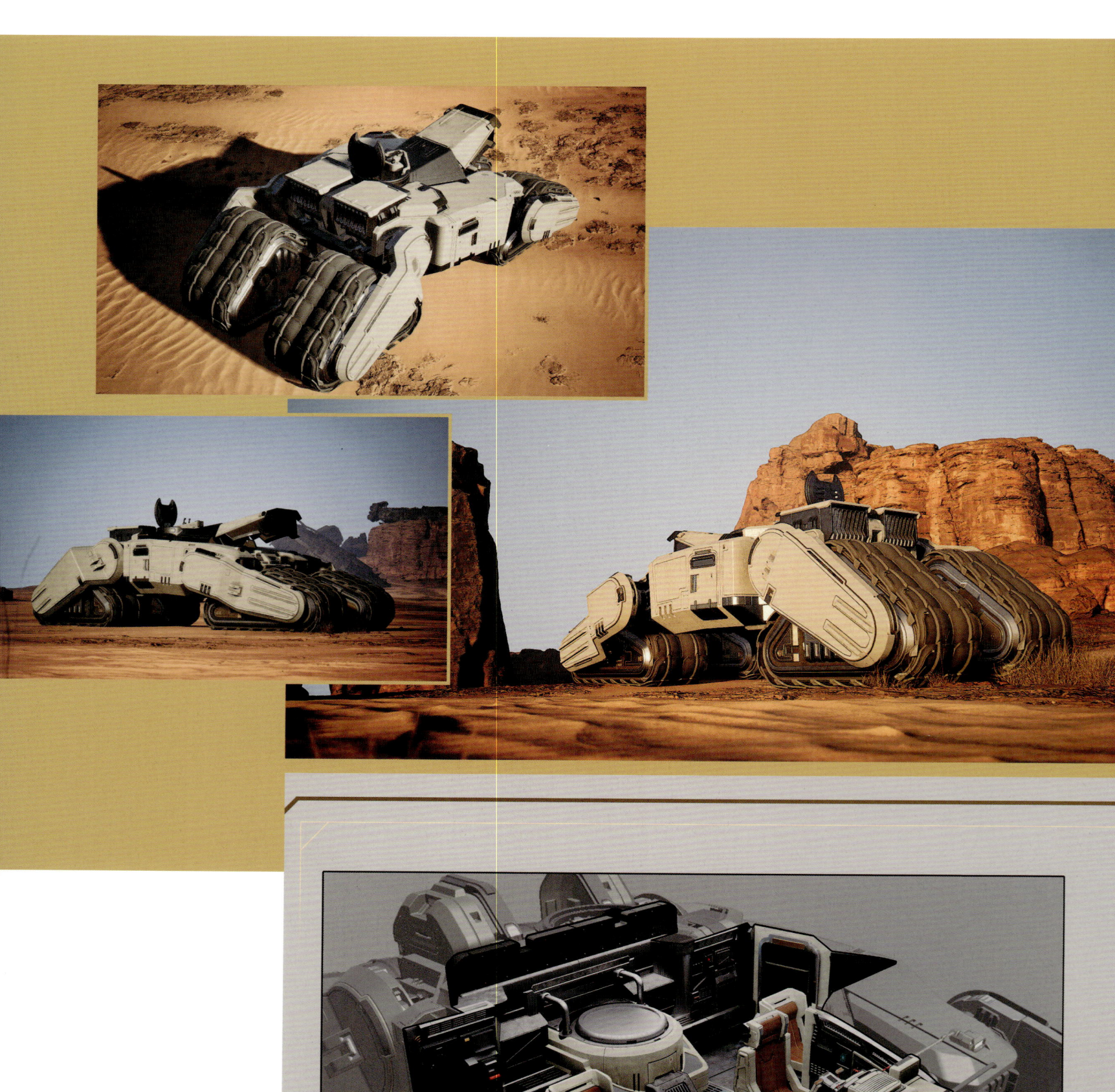

TOP *The CHOAM tank on the sands of Arrakis.*

OPPOSITE TOP *The CHOAM buggy on the sands of Arrakis.*

BOTTOM *CHOAM tank interior design.*

Choam_Tank Interior

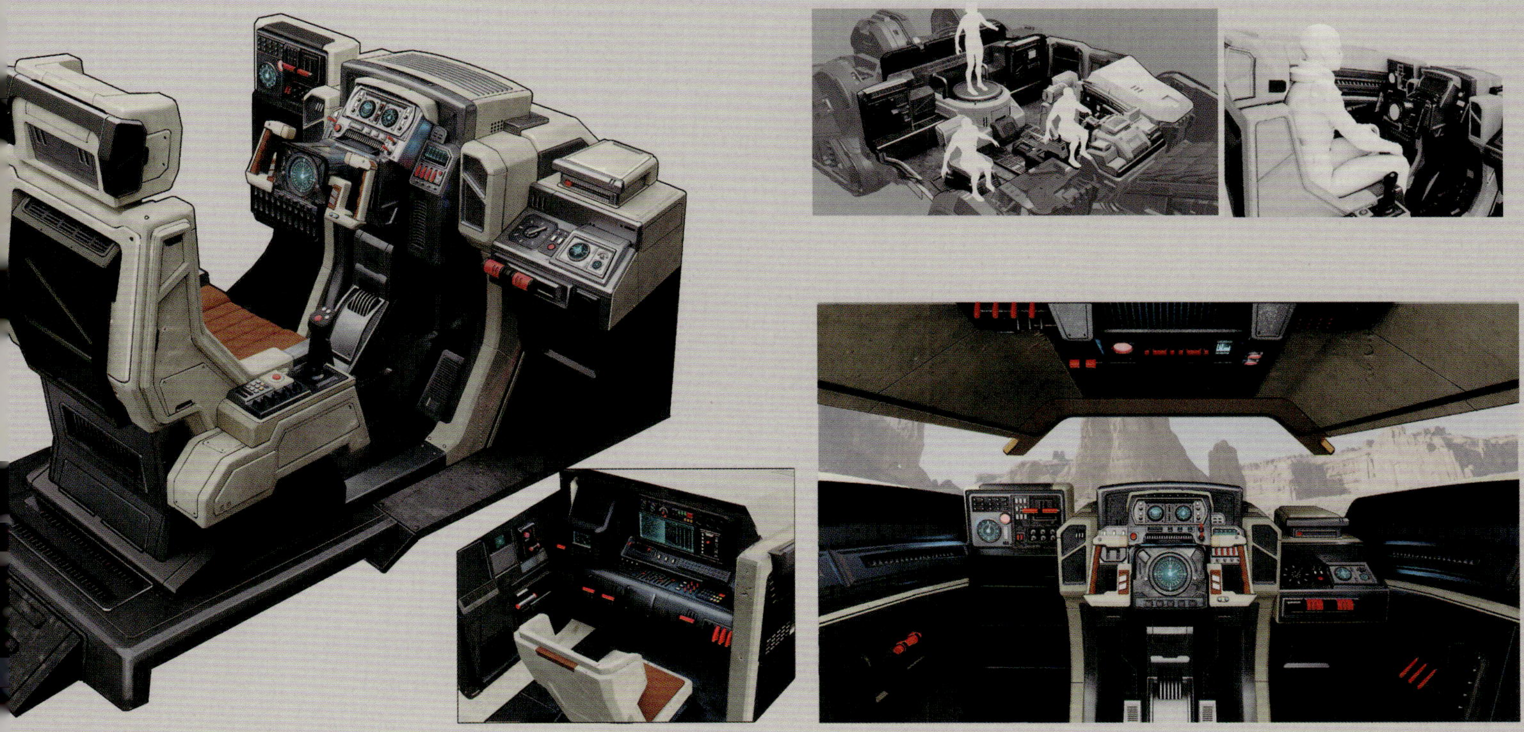

Traversal 169

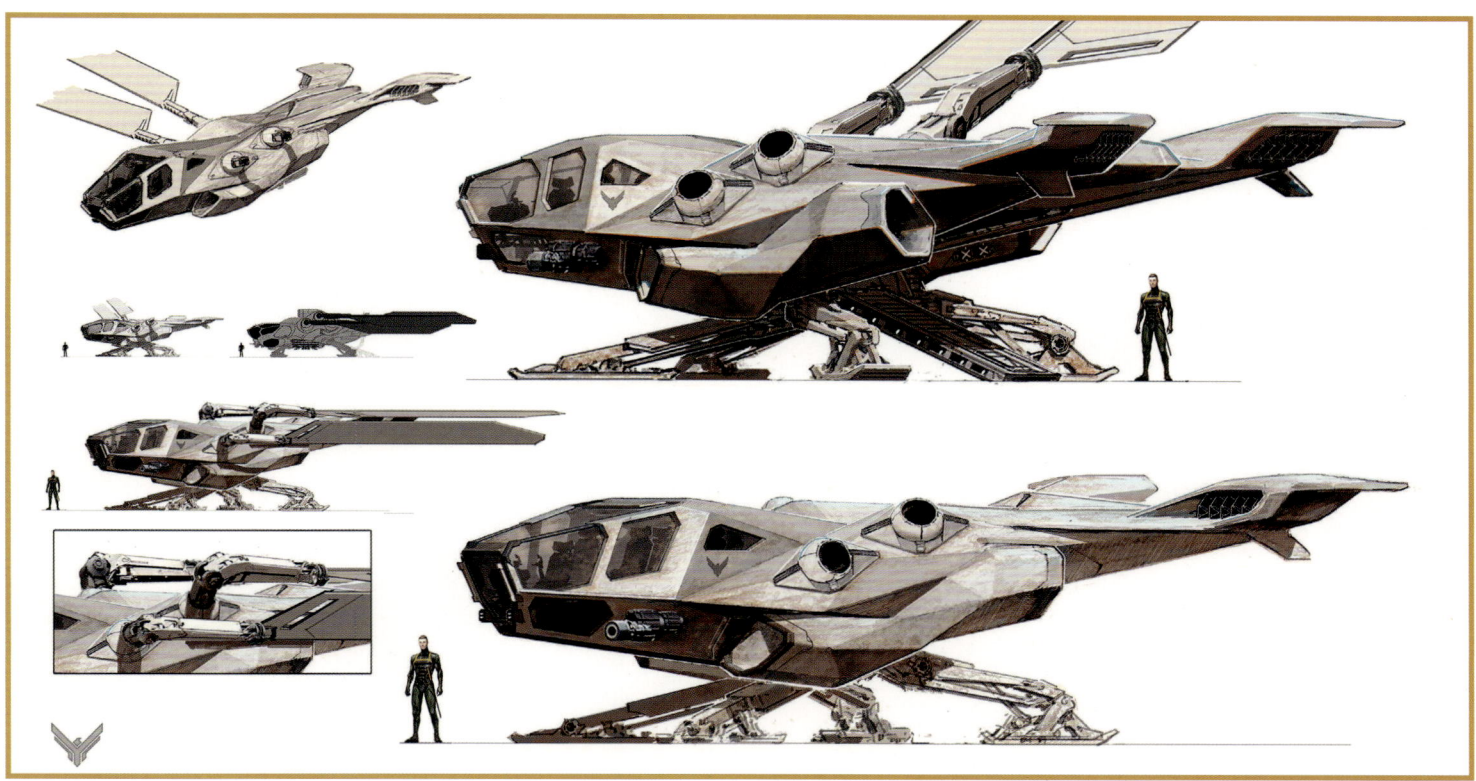

LEARNING TO FLY

The sandbike and dune buggy expand your range considerably from where you can travel on foot, but to realize your full potential, you will have to take to the sky. "Once you're done with all of your ground vehicles, you move up to ornithopters, and you get to explore a lot more of the map," says Froede.

"The ornithopter is the most iconic vehicle in the Dune universe. It's what makes Dune *Dune*. These dragonfly, birdlike vehicles that move with high frequency through the desert. How do we make these look as cool as they did in the movie? We've already seen what an ornithopter can do, but we were very fortunate because Legendary gave us the freedom to really give everything our own take.

"There are some things we took from the movie, because talking with Legendary, some things made sense to adapt directly, but we also had the freedom to find our own way. Things that weren't a one-to-one copy from the movie. An ornithopter should feel very special. It's the first moment in the game where you now have that 360-degree freedom of movement . . . I've always loved games where you can fly. It's always cool. People love flying. We played around with the ornithopter a lot. How can we make it fly and move and look cool and give the player a vehicle that they've been looking forward to using in the game?

OPPOSITE *Unpainted renders of the Atreides light (top) and medium (middle, bottom) ornithopter designs.*

ABOVE *Concept illustrations of the Atreides light ornithopter design.*

"Each faction in the game, Atreides, Harkonnen, has their own version of the ornithopter. You can tell from afar if it's an Atreides ornithopter or a Spacing Guild ornithopter. It's not hard to make it recognizable as a vehicle, since it's got that mechanical body in the middle and these dragonfly wings, and that reads very well from afar. But we had to design that, and to ensure quality performance."

No other vehicle, and perhaps no other aspect of the game, will be under as much scrutiny as the ornithopter, one of the most iconic vehicles in all of science fiction. From their first appearance in the original *Dune* novel by Frank Herbert, who described the ornithopter—or 'thopter, as it's known colloquially—as an aircraft capable of sustained wing-beat flight in the manner of birds, professional illustrators and fans alike rendered their own versions of the ornithopter, and many successful pilots and engineers have drawn inspiration from Frank Herbert and his vision.

LEFT, BELOW *The Atreides light ornithopter on the sands of Arrakis.*

OPPOSITE BOTTOM LEFT *Interior design of the Atreides medium ornithopter.*

OPPOSITE BOTTOM RIGHT *Rear view of the Atreides medium ornithopter shadowed by the Arrakis sunset.*

Traversal

PAGE 174-175 *Unpainted render (top) and concept illustration (bottom) of the Harkonnen light ornithopter design.*

RIGHT *Rear view of the Harkonnen medium ornithopter shadowed by the Arrakis sunset.*

BELOW, OPPOSITE *The Harkonnen light ornithopter on the sands of Arrakis.*

"The ornithopter is, for me, the coolest thing in the game," says longtime Dune enthusiast Barnaby Legg. "What Funcom did with the ornithopter is so exciting. One of the unique opportunities of the game is actually a real challenge. Denis Villeneuve and Patrice Vermette and the entire production team had crafted such a beautiful physicalization of Frank Herbert's book, from the vehicles to the people to the civilization, the architecture . . . We knew the game was going to be inspired by those references, but we also knew the game had to go beyond the films and create a wide range of vehicles and gadgets and costumes, things that we didn't see in the movie. And I think Funcom did a terrific job absorbing the DNA of Denis's vision.

"We were able to meet with the art department and all the heads of department, and Funcom really did a fantastic job absorbing the aesthetic of what Denis was doing in *Dune* and infusing it into all the wonderful things they had to create. The vehicles, the sandbike, all the different land vehicles all of the way up to the ornithopter. We see different models of ornithopter in the films, but Funcom needed to go far beyond that.

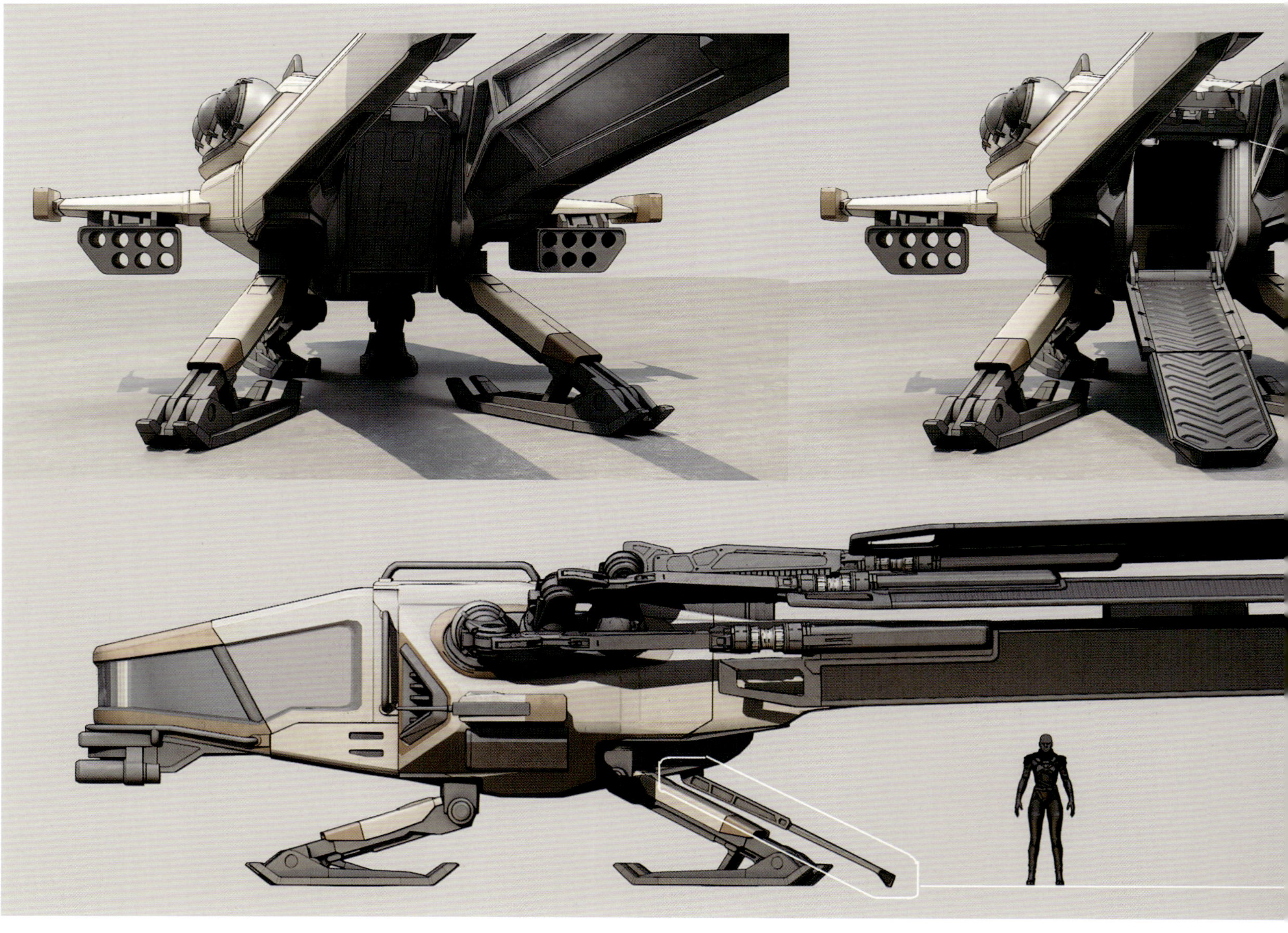

Traversal

"I don't know how many ornithopters there are in the game, but it's a lot. And there are a wide range of different designs, and I think they really embraced the physical sense of realism. There really is a feeling when you see an ornithopter take off onscreen that it's a real thing, no special effects, no wires. You really feel the physicality of those wings and their motion lifting this thing up from the ground. And I really can't wait to see the players once they get into the cockpit of those things. For me, that's the coolest aircraft I've ever seen in science fiction."

Access to the ornithopter opens the map exponentially. Arrakis and all its secrets are now yours to discover. "There is an overland map that, once you get to a certain point in the game and unlock your ornithopter, you're free to fly around and access—almost the entire map of the game, far beyond the initial tutorial area," says Karl Mario Garibay Froede. "The coolest feature is that you can build the ornithopter in your base, then you can jump right in, and you can explore right away. If you see a cave off in the distance, you can set that as your destination. Exploration is so much more with the ornithopter than with the bike.

OPPOSITE TOP *Unpainted render of the CHOAM transport ornithopter design.*

OPPOSITE BOTTOM *Concept illustrations of the CHOAM medium ornithopter design.*

BELOW *Unpainted renders of front and rear views of the CHOAM light ornithopter design.*

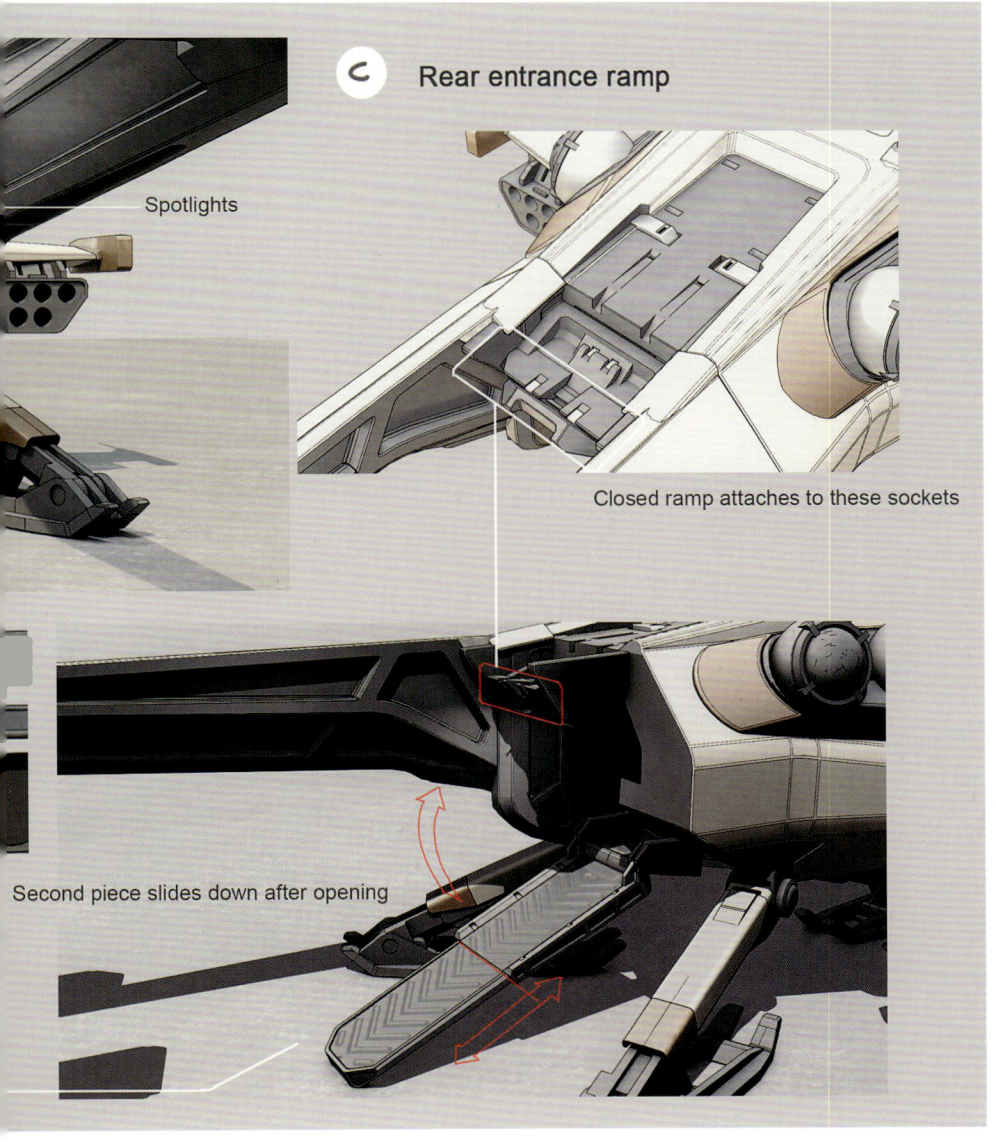

Traversal

"When you are traveling on foot, you have to be very careful moving from one rock island to another. Once you get the bike, it's not that much of an issue anymore, although the sandworm is still faster than you on the bike. But then you get the ornithopter and sandworms aren't as much of a threat, as you can fly right over the terrain. You still have to pay attention to your gas meter; there are still dangerous elements. We're adding some wind tunnels to the game, too, which add an interesting challenge—you can basically save your fuel as you move from one point to another in gliding mode. Turn on the engines, fly and glide, and explore in a way that wasn't available to you before."

That joy of discovery has been at the heart of *Dune: Awakening* from the very first story meeting through the course of its development to the final details and tweaks added by each individual team crafting the survival game. "As a game dev, you hope to work on a project and deliver something special.

Something that players will remember for many years to come. I hope that in twenty years, someone will come to me and say, 'You worked on the *Dune* game! I played the hell out of that, and now my son is playing it, too!' That, for me, is the biggest accomplishment," says Froede. "As an artist, you want to create something special and unique. It's not about fame or standing out, it's about finding something that appeals to players and that they identify with. That does the lore justice. To provide something to the players that they will find interesting, that's the ultimate goal.

"Having battles with dozens of vehicles is a real challenge, and you sometimes have to sacrifice detail for playability, but I'm very pleased with what we've accomplished. I hope that players will be able to see that. We put a lot of thought and a lot of love into these vehicles, and a lot of thought into how they move, how they interact with the world. I think that comes through in the gameplay."

OPPOSITE TOP, ABOVE *The CHOAM light transport ornithopter on the sands of Arrakis.*

OPPOSITE BOTTOM, TOP LEFT *The CHOAM medium ornithopter on the sands of Arrakis.*

TOP RIGHT *The CHOAM transport ornithopter on the sands of Arrakis.*

Traversal

THE NATURE OF THE BEAST

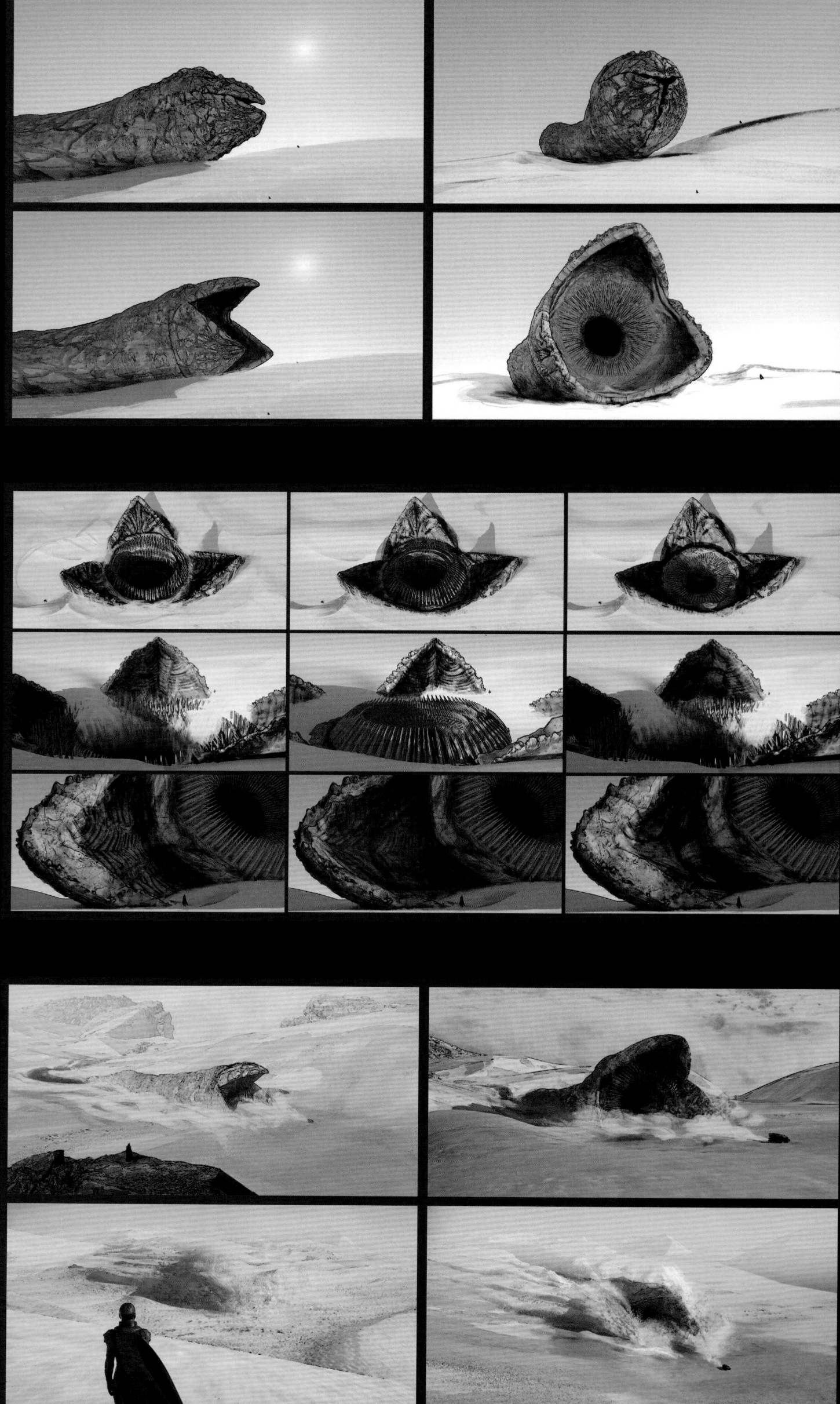

The Arrakis surface holds many perils, from the unforgiving heat to warring factions battling over the planet's precious, limited resources.

But the greatest danger is unseen, hidden below the surface, always moving, always hunting. Sandworms, the giant sand-dwelling creatures native to Arrakis, are sensitive to sound and vibrations on the surface above. An explosion, a deliberate attempt to summon the beast known as Shai-Hulud through technology like the thumper—a short stake with a spring-driven clapper at one end, placed in the sand to "call" sandworms—or even a misstep by someone who has not yet mastered the Fremen skill of walking without rhythm can mean certain death to surface-dwellers. Although the capricious and unpredictable beings known as "Little Maker" or "thing of eternity" may choose to ignore or spare those who live above them if it suits their inscrutable desires, those who live on Arrakis know that it is best not to take that risk.

The Shai-Hulud are inextricably linked to the planet's most valuable resource, the Spice Melange, and those who wish to control Spice must determine if the reward is worth the risk. "Players traveling on the surface risk drawing a sandworm, but there are certain things we've created to draw players out of their comfort zones," says Joel Bylos. "For instance, there's a special kind of sand here on the surface known as flower sand. According to the novels, it's the softest kind of sand, and players can refine it into a variety of different materials that they need for crafting. You must be wary and pay attention, because as you harvest, you risk drawing the attention of the sandworms. Spend too much time in one area and the indicator will warn you that an angry sandworm is coming after you, and the only option is to get back to rocky ground or the sandworm's going to take you."

You will meet your first sandworm almost immediately upon your arrival on Arrakis, after your ship has crashed into the planet's surface. "You learn about the danger of the sandworms right away," says Morgan Sandbæk. "You land on a crashed ornithopter and you get prompted from a voice on the comms, and they tell you basically you need to run to ground *now*. Then you start running, and then we play the animation of the sandworm eating that ornithopter that you crashed in.

"It really sets the tone from the get-go that there's something dangerous out there, and the player is like, 'Oh yeah, but that was just like a normal cinematic event,' and then they get to the rock island. They're on safe ground and they play, do a couple of tutorials. And then when they naturally are supposed to go to the next stage in the game, they might think, 'Oh yeah, I'm just gonna run over the desert, even though they told me not to do it. But I'll just give it a go.' And then you get this moment where the sandworm just sort of reaches up and tells you what's what, but then vanishes in the Deep Desert, the huge, large-scale world that we have. We also have the massive ringmouth sandworm that you see in the *Dune* movies.

"We play this awesome animation where the sandworm breaches up. Particles blow up, almost like pointing at you as a player that, okay, now you're the one in danger. And you have like five to ten seconds to get to safety. If not . . . So that really builds a nice moment for the player. We also have a fake sandworm, which is the first thing that really greets the player once they enter the main map."

PAGES 182-183 *Speed-paint concept art of a sandworm attack.*

OPPOSITE *Early sketches exploring the sandworm's design.*

Once the threat of the sandworm has been established, players learn that their survival will depend on their ability to evade the massive, incredibly powerful leviathans that strike like a force of nature when they break the Arrakis surface. "We have two sandworms in the game," notes Sandbæk. "The one that is revealed early in the gameplay experience makes its presence known as you try to walk or crawl across the open desert by foot. You're going to attract the sandworm because you're making the vibrations in the sand.

"And then we decided to sort of kick it off with this movement. The sandworm really comes up and shows itself for you. Like, 'Here I am! Now you're in danger.'"

That element of danger brings with it a gameplay experience unlike any other: fun but intense, and with high stakes for every player when the Shai-Hulud make their presence known. "Funcom did a great job of sorting out exactly what it would entail if your character were running or riding through the desert, knowing that the sandworm is going to come and will kill you unless you get to the next rock formation or the next protected area," says Sam Rappaport.

"So how do we find the right balance of staying true to the lore and having these 'oh sh*t' moments when you're traversing the desert but also not pissing players off and making it feel like you're constantly just restarting the game?

"If you die at any point in the game during a mission or if you're killed by another player, you have the option of going back to collect items you've lost, and you'll also respawn with a certain percentage of items that you had in your inventory. If you are traversing the desert and you are eaten by a sandworm, you basically lose everything and restart from the beginning. I think that, while occasionally very frustrating, you will have to figure out how to get around the sandworms and will have to be very careful and very strategic about how you are traversing the desert. You can't just go straight from A to Z; you'll have to take a thoughtful approach when studying your map.

"Can I get from here to there before the sandworm gets me? Am I willing to risk my inventory if the sandworm gets me while I'm looking for my next objective or my next resource? When I first started playing the game, it really paid off in those

TOP *Early sketches depicting the scene progression of a sandworm bursting from the sands and devouring an ornithopter.*

OPPOSITE *Sandworm mouth variations.*

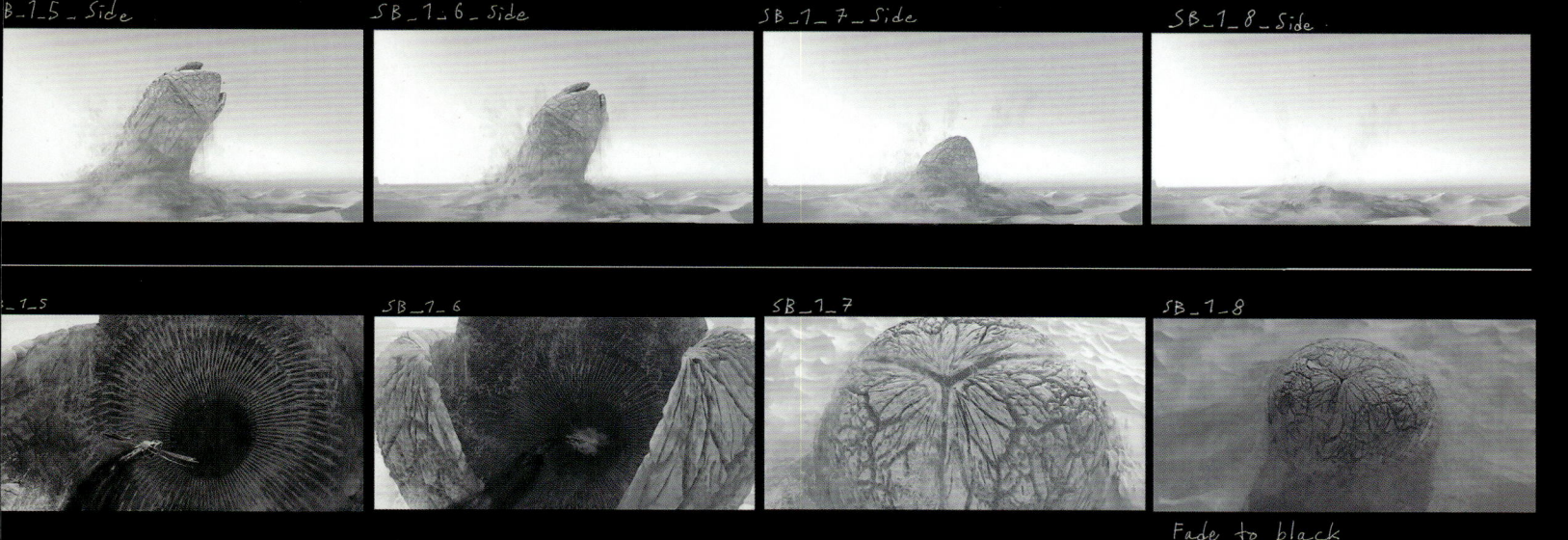

adrenaline-fueled moments with those sandworm attacks, and it was a really fun, exciting mechanic, a great way of organically telling a player that they can't go to a certain section of the map until they rank up and create other ways of traversing."

Those advanced methods of traversal are paramount to your survival. Few can evade the sandworms while traveling on foot. Sandbikes and other ground vehicles will increase your range and your ability to dodge the Shai-Hulud, but only the ornithopter allows you to cross the desert without awakening the dreaded sandworms. Those who can traverse the desert from above will have the greatest advantage when it comes to harvesting the world's most precious resource. "The sandworms are connected to the Spice Blows, these massive Spice Blows," says Morgan Sandbæk. "They flatten the ground. You have a limited time to harvest that Spice before the giant sandworm comes and swallows the whole resource. The whole sort of Spice Blow and everyone that's still in it with their harvesters or, you know, players are battling it out because there's PvP there.

"The sandworm doesn't care. It comes in and grabs everyone as a bunch of different particle effects spawn up.

"You get some warning, and that's when you as a player really need to decide if we should team up and just get the hell out of here, or do we still battle this out? Because if we do, everyone will die, so it's really used to create these tense moments," he concludes. "And it's even more punishing for the player to be killed by a sandworm than by anything else."

The sandworms aren't the only life-forms capable of survival on Arrakis. The desert biome is host to a number of other burrowing animals as well, including the kit fox, kangaroo mouse—or muad'dib—desert hare, and sand terrapin, all of whom do their best to avoid the planet's birds of prey, including the desert hawk, dwarf owl, eagle, and desert owl. A host of deadly arthropods are native to Arrakis as well, including scorpions, centipedes, trapdoor spiders, biting wasps, and wormflies. Although they do pose subtler dangers than the sandworms, nearly every life-form that has adapted to life on Arrakis may pose a threat to every other inhabitant of the desert planet. But the sandworms, obviously, are the apex predators of Arrakis.

The game developers utilized the latest technology to craft sandworms within the world of *Dune: Awakening* that would be as menacing, as deadly, and as unpredictable as the life-forms whose very existence defies belief and defines the lives of everyone on Arrakis. "There's a reason why when people think about Dune, they think about sandworms," says Barnaby Legg. "It's arguably the most iconic monster in all of science fiction. Although calling them monsters is oversimplifying what it is. This creature is a symbiotic god of nature, inherently linked to the Spice.

"One of the things Funcom did was to make it a true living creature in the world. It's not something that only appears in a few pre-canned set pieces animated ahead of time where you just get to witness it passively. The sandworm is out there, alive and in the game world. It's something akin to what you saw Creative Assembly do with the Alien in the *Alien: Isolation* game. These are real AI-driven sandworms. Just as in Dune, if you walk on the sands and create vibrations, the worm will show up and the worm will . . . give you a very bad day. Let's put it that way."

TOP *Desert hare designs.*

MIDDLE *Kit fox designs and iterations.*

LEFT *Growler sandworm.*

The Nature of the Beast 189

THE LONE AND LEVEL SANDS

Arrakis is a desert world. Apart from small rock islands and other natural formations, wreckage from those foolhardy enough to come to this planet, and the occasional isolated city or shelter, the dominant features of the landscape are the sand dunes, the seemingly infinite sand dunes.

But as with the planet itself, once one is immersed in the world and its culture, there is considerably more to Arrakis than meets the eye. "Since my time on *Conan Exiles*, my career has been sand. Sand, sand, sand, and rocks," says Morgan Sandbæk, Associate Technical Art Director at Funcom. "*Dune: Awakening* was literally quite barren when I joined the team, as the game's first art director left the project. Then we brought in a new one, and that sort of shifted the visuals towards more like it is today. And it felt a bit more raw, even harsh to some degree. We were exploring lighting and mood, and we hadn't settled on the atmosphere and the sort of colors and the tone and temperature. A lot of that was still up in prototyping and researching. We had a bunch of awesome concepts, but some of them didn't translate to a full day-night cycle.

"A lot of the moods were kind of exploratory, like strongly saturated or really cool for a concept, but then you're trying to blend daytime sort of lighting and then they go into nighttime and it has some colors that are completely not complementary, and they don't translate well to each other. We've been through a lot of iterations on that. We're also playing with the shapes of the dunes. The size and the scale of traversal, the density of playable area. So yeah, it was quite barren. It was a different game at that point in time as well."

PAGES 190-191, OPPOSITE, LEFT *Concept art of the deteriorated factory in the Red Desert of the Vermilius Gap, featuring a darker, harsher art style.*

ABOVE *Exploration of an Arrakis desert landscape.*

PAGES 196-197 LEFT *Early exploration of an Arrakis landscape covered in evening primrose.*

PAGES 196-197 RIGHT *Concept art studying the construction of an environmental shelter.*

The Lone and Level Sands

THE LONG AND WINDING ROAD

The dunes hold many secrets. Arrakis was not always a desert. Newcomers are surprised to discover that the blistering daytime heat gives way to freezing cold when night falls, but will learn the time-tested ways if they hope to survive.

It fell to Morgan Sandbæk and his team to capture the surprising depth and diversity of the lone and level sands. "It's been a really long journey. We quickly realized that we don't have a lot of things to work with. We have the sand. We have the rocks, and sort of you have a couple of different shrubs. That's it. Sandstone, sand, and dry grass. Then you really have to work with the different color balance between things and the nuances, and you're trying to build shapes into the shape, if that makes sense.

"If you look at the landscape, the sand dunes, it's not one hue of sand. It's a lot of different colors blending in and out, and we put a great effort into having the ability to basically paint and recolorize the sand across the whole landscape without putting in super-large textures, just blowing up the video memory," Sandbæk continues. "But you still want to have that direction. You want to show the shapes, and you want to emphasize them, and you want to blend in some different colors where you can. And if you're just taking the traditional approach and you just apply textures and it's a sand texture, that's nice, but when you have eight-by-eight kilometers of that, it quickly becomes repetitive. We've been through a lot of different approaches, everything from [procedural software] Houdini, doing everything like simulating the different shapes and then pulling in large-scale textures. It's been a long journey, but we settled on a sort of erosion-based simulation. We take the environment into Houdini. We run simulations on it to see how things would flow, and then we apply a color tint based on that. It's more the shapes and the moods that you get into the screen—you really need to try to play on emotions a bit more because you don't have things to hide behind.

TOP *Exploration of desert textures and rock formations.*

BOTTOM *Concept art of evening primrose, one of the natural resources in the game.*

The Lone and Level Sands

"We can't just put up a forest and sort of say, here's a bunch of random trees and rocks. They look natural because it's chaotic by nature. It's like, here's an open field. You have a rock island. And that's the thing you look at, and then the environment team has done a tremendous job shaping that to make it interesting, you know, have overarching shapes that sort of pique interest to the player. We tried to do like a fully procedural way where we sort of covered the landscape in clips, but that only got us, you know, seventy or eighty percent coverage. But you really need the artist touch; you need people to come in, give intent to the shape, and make it unique and interesting. Basically, you want to make players investigate these places, visit them. It's been a big team effort to put it that way."

It is said that variety is the spice of life, and that is especially true when one is confronted with an infinite landscape that could very easily fall into a vast, endless expanse of desert sand. Without that variety, players will lose focus and find themselves disengaged from the gameplay, and from the game itself. "A lot of that comes from the art direction, of course," says Sandbæk. "We are fortunate to have a brilliant art director, Gavin Whelan, who helps us to make the right decisions. And that translates into having some nice colors in the world. Yes, Arrakis is supposed to be scorching hot and dangerous. And you're getting punished by being in the sun. But if you do that one hundred percent of the time, the players will quit after ten minutes because their eyes are starting to be drier from the light from the screen.

ABOVE *Some of the minable resources found in-game, including erythrite (left), carbon (top right), and copper (bottom right).*

OPPOSITE *More minable resources, including another erythrite variant (top) and jasmium (bottom).*

The Lone and Level Sands

"So we introduce some peak times during the day when it's the most intense, but then we also direct it to sort of settle down and give players a bit more breathing room, a bit more time to sort of absorb and observe the environment, and we also put a lot of emphasis into the nighttime to make that the calm before the storm. You get more blues. You have a nice contrast to the red or warm daytime. You pull auroras into the sky so we can play with a lot more colors and create some weirdness, and you get these pockets of lights.

"That should pique some interest. And then the daytime comes again. And you're into that survival loop where you sort of say, 'Okay, I need to stay in the shade.' It's super hot out there, you see, when the sun hits the sand, and it causes heat distortion and almost blows out the screen when you hit it like at a perfect angle to be pure white," he continues. "And then, of course, you play with post-processing to create some bloom depending on where you are in different full-screen effects to convey different dangers or effects that might affect the player, or the character, and we need to make sure that the player understands what the character is going through."

Those who live on the planet know that only fools underestimate the perils of Arrakis, and only those who truly understand the desert, who are able to learn its secrets, will thrive here. "Arrakis is Arrakis and the desert takes the weak. This is my desert. My Arrakis. My Dune," said Baron Harkonnen, announcing that although he would not harm the House Atreides directly, the desert would surely dispatch any offworlders who dared to defy it.

LET THERE BE LIGHT

"My planet, Arrakis, is so beautiful when the sun is low. Rolling over the sands, you can see Spice in the air," spoke Chani Kynes of the Fremen, in admiration of the natural beauty of Arrakis, an aspect of that world that few can fully appreciate.

"It's almost like the third actor, just like you have the environment and then you have the characters and then you have the lighting, in my mind," says Morgan Sandbæk. "It really makes everything shine to have the correct moods. It emphasizes when it plays well with the story beat. It of course enhances it, and we're trying to go for this realistic, harsh environment, but we also need to have the nice moments. The more natural, familiar mood. We built a biome system that lets us take a region in the world and apply a different mood and atmosphere in that region, and then when the player moves out of that, it fades into whatever the new mood and atmospherics and post-processing [are], et cetera.

"That, like the color tones, should be something we use a lot to complement the simple environment that we have, which is the desert. How do you make a brown desert look different? You can try a different mood on it to sort of tint it slightly differently because it's different weather or a different story beat. You're going to see a lot of different color temperatures depending on where you are in the game—if you're in a crashed spaceship, an imperial testing station, or roaming around in the desert; it's even different regions in the desert. It's one of the key elements to create variation for us."

Bringing that variation to light was the responsibility of Associate Art Director David Levy. He and his team bridged the gap between Dune's live-action and video game productions, which created a symbiotic, organic relationship between the two worlds. "I worked on the television series *Dune: Prophecy* before joining the *Dune: Awakening* team. At first, I was hired as a lead for anything that was 'hard-surfaced,' like weapons and anything technological. Then I was put into the lead of the lighting department, which was a massive undertaking. Lighting for a game with many different platforms, many different video cards, is very complex.

TOP *Concept art of the Red Desert megafactory.*
BOTTOM *Ground level of the Red Desert megafactory.*

ABOVE, OPPOSITE
Biological imperial testing station explorations.

"It was made easier thanks to the help of the lighting system Lumen, but at the same time there were many technical difficulties in making this work on all platforms," says Levy. "It was really a massive task. We started from the ground up, deciding what kind of mood the game will have, and how closely we will adhere to the movie versus our own vision for what Dune is. If we did only one type of atmosphere or mood, that would not be enough variety for the player. We want to maintain their interest throughout the game. Interiors, exteriors, making these transitions seamless . . . Let's say that you are outside, then you have to run quickly inside an area; you'll have to wait a moment as you adjust to the change in light quality and exposure.

"Because this is really an open-world game, where you can go in and out of buildings . . . technically, it creates a huge number of challenges, but we were able to handle that thanks to our skilled creative team, and thanks to Gavin Whelan's art direction and the great lighting team that we were able to put together."

Dune: Awakening took its overall art direction and its visual cues from the cinematic world established by Denis Villeneuve and Patrice Vermette, but there were many challenges that were unique to the fully immersive, explorable Arrakis faced by the game development team that were not part of the live-action team's process. "We have very distinctive zones throughout the game, each very independent, visually," says Levy. "Influenced by the redness of the sun, or the rocks. Some influenced by the amount of toxicity in the area. Whether it's on foot or in a vehicle or flying, you must be able to navigate between those areas and change those moods seamlessly without disrupting the gameplay. We had to make those transitions happen nicely and artfully between different areas of the game.

"The mantra that we had all through the company was 'use the movie as a base.' Especially for lighting. Then we can extrapolate from there. There were some areas in the movie that were very saturated, very warm, and that worked great for us as a base for determining the lighting at twelve o'clock. But the game is not just noon—it's everything from dusk 'til dawn. Everything from six a.m. all the way through midnight, so we needed to include every variation, and we translated the twelve o'clock from the movie and we had to extrapolate things like what would the air, and the particles in it, do as the position of the sun changed throughout the day? How does the desert look under moonlight? From that base, we could see Arrakis at different times of day, and that was a great challenge.

"There are not many games that do this, but we were able to create variations for every single day that you experience in the game. Every day has slight variations. Colors, temperatures, dust in the air. Every time you go to a new area of the game, you're not just experiencing that location but a different feeling, look, and atmosphere, every single day.

"Even in a desert, there are so many natural things happening. The amount of dust in the air. Pollution. Cliffs, rocks . . . almost an infinite number of creative choices apart from just endless sand. There were so many ways to interpret the desert."

And that interpretation makes *Dune: Awakening* both a part of the greater Dune universe and apart from the greater Dune universe. "Just to figure out the basic daytime lighting took a lot of trial and error. After a long while, we were able to nail down the 'Arrakis essence,'" says Levy. "The basic day-to-day lighting is fantastic. The far regions are very cinematic and echo the look of the films."

CHARTING THE COURSE

Ensuring that the *Dune: Awakening* universe complements that of Denis Villeneuve's films is the responsibility of Gavin Whelan, Funcom's Senior Art Director. "Essentially, we've got a large pool of artists, and each group has an individual lead and individual art director who's in charge. My role is to be in charge of those leads, to be the one voice who makes the visual decisions," says Whelan. "Legendary is involved from the movie side, to make sure that we're true to the films, but we also need to be true to the books and to be true to the game requirements. The creative director sits right behind me, and I'm the first person who gets told if something's incorrect, if we're not following the lore in the books.

"The pressure to be more cinematic has increased, especially when you're working on a game like *Dune: Awakening*, collaborating with a team who has won Oscars®, on properties that have Denis Villeneuve and Greig Fraser working on them, and you've got to do something that, in some way, holds on to that, connects to that. It's scary at first," he admits. "But talking to Greig Fraser, who's brilliant, like a lot of people who work in movies or games, at the heart, they just love what they do. And it doesn't take long before that comes through, and it's just two guys talking about films and visuals at a certain point. Sharing cool ideas. So that's that."

Whelan's introduction to *Dune* came in 1984, with the release of David Lynch's film adaptation of Frank Herbert's novel. That and his exposure to fantasy art and book covers on display at sci-fi bookstores in his native Dublin laid the foundation for both his Dune fandom and his gaming career. "Dune was always there. Always the pinnacle of what sci-fi novels could be. To get the chance to work on Dune was scary, honestly. In adapting it, a lot of people have succeeded, but a lot of people have failed to bring Dune to life. But Denis Villeneuve did such a great job of bisecting it and separating the parts into a story that would be suitable for a twenty-first-century audience. Something that would bring in existing fans but also attract mainstream people, to be able to please both, that's really hard to do. He deserves the praise he gets for that.

"The game allows us to do some of the weirder stuff. We looked at the classic book illustrations from the sixties and seventies and tried to bring that vibrancy and life to it. As a story, it's special, and I tell this to all the artists as we're working on the project. This sort of project doesn't come around often. A lot of games can be very generic. *Star Wars* has such a strong influence on sci-fi that there's a lot that can be tracked back to that concept art. But we have a chance with *Dune* to do something unique.

"I keep telling our concept artists how privileged we are to work on this, and that I don't use that lightly," he continues. "I've worked on a lot of important licenses in the past, but this one stands apart. It's very different from anything else out there. It has very interesting themes, and it's very hard to convey some of the strangeness. There's so much scope, and we're only scratching the surface. We've got so many characters and concepts that we're looking to explore in the future as well. To pull

ABOVE *Landscape exploration of Arrakis at sunset.*

what's unique about the books and to put that on the screen, that's the challenge. It's a real honor to work on this."

Thanks to trailblazers like Frank Herbert, George Lucas, and David Lynch, the groundwork was in place for a filmmaker like Villeneuve to find a receptive audience for his vision of *Dune*, according to Whelan. "Each medium has its own challenges and pressures and limitations when it comes to telling stories. When you're making a television show, you've got a budget, and if you're trying to tell a massive story on a tiny budget, it's going to be a challenge. You're targeting as wide an audience as possible to make the project viable. Gameplayers, maybe the current audience, are more adaptable to unusual things. We have such breadth now. Growing up in the eighties, we'd have a limited number of television shows available to us, as selected by a small group of people, but now the internet has widened what's out there exponentially. Anything goes. It's a very strange place. People are producing their own content now. It's not as funneled as it used to be.

"We have the possibility to present the weird and unusual to the player, and they understand it," he continues. "They understand the universe that we're trying to show to them, and we're not limited to just that small percentage of people that have read the book. The general audience's palate is wider now, and they're seeing more things. Maybe the audience has changed dramatically as well, over the past several decades. My kids, for example, are much more adaptable when it comes to new content than my generation. It's going to be interesting. If we're courageous, if we're not just focused on making generic games and repeated games, we can push the boundaries of what entertainment is, and we'll keep expanding those horizons."

TOP *Early concept art exploring an Arrakis desert field covered in evening primrose, shown at night (right) and during the day (below).*

Dune: Awakening and the *Dune* films both make a point of providing a gradual introduction to the more fantastic elements of Frank Herbert's universe, grounding the audience through relatable characters and technology before expanding their horizons. "The films did so many things really well," Whelan observes. "If you think about ornithopters, the descriptions in the book, they were quite literally dragonflies there and in most visual depictions that followed. Villeneuve took that and made it believable, made it tangible, and that was important to ground the world into something more realistic and relatable. He didn't want to just explain it by calling it 'space magic.'

"*Star Wars* was like a World War II movie, with fighter jets, good guys, and bad guys; they made it very easy to understand. Villeneuve was using a much more complicated story, but he still had to have that footprint to make it believable. The mechanics of the machinery had to be completely understandable and real, but in some ways, like looking at the big ships and how they moved without sound . . . that was almost godlike, almost magical. But real. They found that balance between providing technology that was understandable and relatable but also came from so far in the future that we've no idea how it works. He got that balance perfectly correct.

"Within that scope, there's so much that we can do. The suspensor technology, the way it's portrayed in the movie, was very simple, but we could do so many things with it, once you introduce that hovering and flying ability. We can incorporate it into almost anything—vehicles, furniture, movement. Villeneuve and Legendary did an incredible job with that, building this into a believable

The Lone and Level Sands

universe for the viewers, that they could buy into, and then introducing the strange and the unusual. And some of the themes were very, very human. It needs to work on multiple levels, and Villeneuve and they did a very good job understanding the source material and bringing it to a wider audience."

With that framework established, Whelan notes, *Dune: Awakening* has the potential to explore every aspect of life on Arrakis . . . and far beyond its dunes, as well. "With the gameplay, with the vehicles . . . as the player expands and increases their abilities, they get access to a wider world as they become more powerful. The way we discover and expand our horizons, literally.

"At the start of the game, you're on the lowest rung of the ladder. There are creatures on the world who are higher up the chain than you. And you're on foot, trying to stay out of the sun, trying to drink water from plants, just trying to survive the next few days. And, step by step, you learn. You manage. You build. You increase your power to the point where you have an ornithopter and you're flying. Traversal. The small steps become larger and more significant. You can travel in seconds what would have previously taken you hours. The scale of the world opens up exponentially. It's the beauty of the mechanics involved. We're going to just keep building and expanding and making the gameplay bigger and more expansive. The way games are now, we can do this; we can keep building and expanding.

"I tell people in the press, we've got a Heighliner [starship] in the sky, and it's a shame not to use it," Whelan hints. "What planets can we go to in the future? We need to make sure we funnel players together, since it's a multiplayer experience and we can't just separate everyone across the universe. But Caladan is interesting. Giedi Prime is really interesting. Where can we send the player in the future away from Arrakis? But the gravity, the importance of Arrakis—that will always pull the player back to it. Control the Spice, control the universe.

"This is exciting and scary at the same time," Whelan admits. "So sometimes, I don't realize until I look at the full scope of what we're trying to produce, all the artwork we've worked on over the years. And we've only really scratched the surface of what we can produce, what we will produce. I can see us widening out, climbing into an ornithopter to see the universe as we can present it. Just getting bigger and bigger. It doesn't diminish in interest, it never gets stale or boring, it will just keep getting bigger, and I think that's perfect for the kind of game we're trying to make.

"As game developers, we're always trying to make an alternative reality for players to go to visit. A lot of people, they have day jobs, they work, they go to school . . . they need an escape. And the more interesting and diverse that we can make it, the more value it has for people. We want to create an experience for the players that's as big as the world can be, and I think *Dune: Awakening* has the potential to be absolutely massive. Technical limitations held games like this back in the past, but we're transcending those limitations every day. Part of my job is to keep our team in check. They're like a team of energetic, wild horses, and I've got to rein them in and keep them from going off in all directions. The passion is consistent across the team. Everyone wants to make this great."

ARRAKIS ASCENDANT

Environmental cataclysm. Scarcity of natural resources that we once took for granted. Corrupt politicians abusing the system and their own people to consolidate their wealth and power. Class warfare. Science versus religion. Fierce debate over the usage and the morality of artificial intelligence in our culture. Heritage. Immigration. Assimilation. The role of women in society. Fate versus free will. Individualism versus collectivism. The generation gap. Colonialism. Exploitation.

Six decades after its original publication, *Dune* is as timeless and perhaps more relevant than ever, as meaningful to young people today as Frank Herbert's novel was when it first captured the public's imagination in 1965. Those themes that made *Dune* one of the most beloved and most popular science-fiction novels of all time have also established the foundation upon which an entire extended universe of novels, films, television series, graphic novels, and video games was built. "Science fiction is always a metaphor for our day-to-day struggles," says Funcom's David Levy. "Dune is able to encompass so many things that are part of today's society. The world is so alien to ours, yet so universal."

It is that universality that informs the alternate world of *Dune: Awakening*, and that the developers hope will bring together gamers around the world as they explore Arrakis and learn its mysteries together in a game that captures the breadth and the spirit of the novels and other creative works that inspired it. "From my perspective, the goal has always been to make the game feel authentically Dune," says Joel Bylos of Funcom. "If you've seen or read any version of Dune, you'll feel that this feels atmospherically and spiritually like a Dune project. That it doesn't feel like it can be anything [else] that has a desert. That we paid attention to all these details from the books.

PAGES 210-211 *Concept sketch exploring the Arrakis desert biome.*

OPPOSITE *Concept art of some of the various imperial testing stations found across the Arrakis desert.*

"I hope people feel that it's an authentic take on the Dune universe. And I hope that people who have read the books find something of value in the fact that we've done this alternate history, that it sits beside the other stuff. Not a new canon. The canon exists, and it's strong. We've made a story that's interesting but doesn't change what you love about the franchise. That would be my hope.

"And then, of course, I just hope that people like it. That's obviously the number one thing, right? I hope that people find the sandworms as terrifying as they should find the sandworms. I hope that they feel like the big iconic moments of the books and the movies are captured in the game in their own ways."

The initial release of *Dune: Awakening* is just the first step in what the game developers expect will be a long, collaborative journey between the creative team and the players who, they hope, will embrace this new chapter of the Dune mythos as readily as they did Denis Villeneuve's films. New characters, new secrets, and new abilities will be revealed . . . in time, according to Bylos. "When we reach the point in the game where the players encounter the Fremen, actually encounter them, for real—the official line is that the Fremen are gone, but from the start of the game we cast doubt on that, since your mission is to find the Fremen—they will gain access to some of the more iconic things that they didn't have access to, since they were just untrained people."

"Things like walking without rhythm on the sand. Or things that a lot of people want in the game that we don't have yet, like riding the sandworm. This is something that we're working toward in the future. The movie did it so well, *Part Two* did it so extremely well that it's going to be difficult to capture in gameplay, that sense of something truly epic. That's something that I have to spend a lot of time thinking about right now."

OPPOSITE *Imperial testing station concept art.*

Arrakis Ascendant 215

"Just as your character's survival is dependent upon your ability to adapt and evolve as you progress through the world of Arrakis, the game itself will adapt and evolve over time, a prospect that the game developers find equal parts thrilling and terrifying," says Sam Rappaport of Legendary Entertainment. "The hope is that *Dune: Awakening* comes out and everyone loves it from the outset, although it's meant to be a living, breathing machine," he continues. "Aside from player feedback that I'm sure we'll get, especially for a live service title, one of the things that makes those games, in my opinion, much more interesting from a developer perspective is that you're really listening to the audience and tweaking things on the fly, or as close to on the fly as possible, and it's really meant to last a long time. As we come out with more content on the linear side, of course we'll try to bring all that look and feel into the game whenever possible. To not just mirror but to expand on the franchise and the lore through the game.

"And we truly think that there's something for everyone in the game. Easter eggs for hardcore Dune fans. You can level up and become a Paul Atreides and try to rule Arrakis. If you're a casual gamer, you can explore the map and engage in the basics of the lore. You can get something from this no matter what your level of familiarity with Dune."

OPPOSITE *Imperial testing station concept art.*

ABOUT THE AUTHOR

Andrew Farago is the curator of San Francisco's Cartoon Art Museum and the author of *Batman: The Definitive History of the Dark Knight in Comics, Film, and Beyond, DC: Collecting the Multiverse: The Art of Sideshow*, and the Harvey Award–winning *Teenage Mutant Ninja Turtles: The Ultimate Visual History*. In 2015, he received the prestigious Inkpot Award from Comic-Con International.

TOP, OPPOSITE
Imperial testing station concept art.

FRANK HERBERT

Frank Herbert (1920–1986) created the most beloved novel in the annals of science fiction, *Dune*. He was a man of many facets, of countless passageways that ran through an intricate mind. His magnum opus reflects this, a classic work that stands as one of the most complex, multilayered novels ever written in any genre. Today, the novel is more popular than ever, with new readers continually discovering it and telling their friends to pick up a copy. It has been translated into dozens of languages and has sold tens of millions of copies worldwide, in more than forty languages.

As a child growing up in Washington State, Frank Herbert was curious about everything. He carried around a Boy Scout pack with books in it, and he was always reading. He loved Rover Boys' adventures, as well as the stories of H. G. Wells, Jules Verne, and the science fiction of Edgar Rice Burroughs. On his eighth birthday, Frank stood on top of the breakfast table at his family home and announced, "I wanna be a author." His curiosity and independent spirit got him into trouble more than once when he was growing up and caused him difficulties as an adult as well. He did not graduate from college because he refused to take the required courses for a major; he only wanted to study what interested him. For years, he had a hard time making a living, bouncing from job to job and from town to town. He was so independent that he refused to write for a particular market; he wrote what he felt like writing. It took him five years of research and writing to complete *Dune*, and after all that struggle and sacrifice, twenty-three publishers rejected it in book form before it was finally accepted. He received an advance of only $7,500.

His loving wife of thirty-seven years, Beverly, was the breadwinner much of the time, as an underpaid advertising writer for department stores. Having been divorced from his first wife, Flora Parkinson, Frank Herbert met Beverly Stuart in a University of Washington creative writing class in 1946. At the time, they were the only students in the class who had sold their work for publication. Frank had sold two pulp adventure stories to magazines, one to *Esquire* and the other to *Doc Savage*. Beverly had sold a story to *Modern Romance* magazine. These genres reflected the interests of the two young lovers; he the adventurer, the strong outdoorsman, and she the romantic, feminine and soft-spoken.

Their long marriage would produce two sons, Brian, born in 1947, and Bruce, born in 1951. Frank also had a daughter, Penny, born in 1942 from his first marriage. For more than two decades, Frank and Beverly would struggle to make ends meet, and there were many hard times. To pay the bills and to allow her husband the freedom he needed to create, Beverly gave up her creative writing career in order to support his. They were a writing team, as he discussed every aspect of his stories with her, and she edited his work. Theirs was a remarkable, though tragic, love story—which Brian would poignantly describe one day in *Dreamer of Dune*. After Beverly passed away, Frank married Theresa Shackelford.

In all, Frank Herbert wrote nearly thirty popular books and collections of short stories, including six novels set in the Dune universe: *Dune*, *Dune Messiah*, *Children of Dune*, *God Emperor of Dune*, *Heretics of Dune*, and *Chapterhouse: Dune*. All were international bestsellers, as were a number of his other science-fiction novels, including *The White Plague* and *The Dosadi Experiment*.

For the complete biography of Frank Herbert, read *Dreamer of Dune* by Brian Herbert.

OPPOSITE, LEFT
Concept art exploring the construction of a Harkonnen building set.

ABOVE *Frank Herbert portrait by Greg Manchess.*

PAGES 222-223
Landscape exploration of the Vermillius Gap.

Published by Titan Books, London, in 2025

TITAN BOOKS

A division of Titan Publishing Group Ltd
144 Southwark Street
London SE1 0UP
www.titanbooks.com

Find us on Facebook: www.facebook.com/TitanBooks
Follow us on Instagram: @titanbooks

© TM & © 2025 Legendary. All rights reserved.
Introduction by Brian Herbert, Kevin J. Anderson, Byron Merritt, and Kim Herbert copyright © Herbert Properties LLC.

INSIGHT EDITIONS

Published by arrangement with Insight Editions, San Rafael, California. www.insighteditions.com

No part of this publication may be reproduced, stored in a retrieval system, or transmitted, in any form or by any means without the prior written permission of the publisher, nor be otherwise circulated in any form of binding or cover other than that in which it is published and without a similar condition being imposed on the subsequent purchaser.

A CIP catalogue record for this title is available from the British Library.

EU RP (for authorities only)
eucomply OÜ Pärnu mnt 139b-14 11317, Talinn, Estonia
hello@eucompliancepartner.com +3375690241

ISBN: 9781835416501

Publisher: Raoul Goff
SVP, Group Publisher: Vanessa Lopez
VP, Creative: Chrissy Kwasnik
VP, Manufacturing: Alix Nicholaeff
Publishing Director: Mike Degler
Art Director: Catherine San Juan
Junior Designer: Samuel Louie
Executive Editor: Jennifer Sims
Senior Editor: Eric Geron
Assistant Editor: Alecsander Zapata
Managing Editor: Nora Milman
Senior Production Manager: Greg Steffen
Strategic Production Planner: Lina s Palma-Temena

Text by Andrew Farago
Design support by Malea Clark-Nicholson

Insight Editions, in association with Roots of Peace, will plant two trees for each tree used in the manufacturing of this book. Roots of Peace is an internationally renowned humanitarian organization dedicated to eradicating land mines worldwide and converting war-torn lands into productive farms and wildlife habitats. Roots of Peace will plant two million fruit and nut trees in Afghanistan and provide farmers there with the skills and support necessary for sustainable land use.

Manufactured in China by Insight Editions

10 9 8 7 6 5 4 3 2 1